Past Present

LIVING WITH HEIRLOOMS AND ANTIQUES

SUSAN SULLY

The Monacelli Press

Past Present

LIVING WITH HEIRLOOMS AND ANTIQUES

SUSAN SULLY

The Monacelli Press

Contents

Introduction

The most inspiring houses are filled with pieces that are carefully chosen, personally meaningful, and thoughtfully displayed. Whether decorated with heirlooms that have been cherished by generations or collected objects that reveal the personal taste and passions of their present-day owners, such houses are intriguing, engaging, and satisfying on many levels. Antiques add the touch of time and the human hand, creating an ambiance impossible to imitate with newly manufactured things. We love old furniture and silver for the depth and beauty of its patina, acquired through years of use, perhaps a bit of misuse, and endless dusting and polishing. Every dented baby cup, mended tablecloth, perfectly or imperfectly preserved piece of glass or porcelain tells a story that began long ago and hasn't ended yet. They are tangible reminders of people, places, or times that may be distant or gone, but they are also treasures to be enjoyed in the present.

This book is about the objects that come to us, the ones we choose, and the way we integrate them into our lives. Contemporary English artist Damien Hirst recently wrote, "I think of a collection as being like a map of someone's life, like the flotsam and jetsam washed up on the beach of someone's existence." While there is certainly flotsam and jetsam randomness to the things we inherit and even those discovered at flea markets, antiques shops, and auctions, there is also a degree of choice. The things with which we surround ourselves express personal values, interests, and aesthetics. They speak volumes about who we are and the lives we have lived. The same is true of the way we live with them. Do we tuck our heirlooms away in attics and cabinets? Are our most cherished possessions relegated to formal rooms where little time is spent? Or do we integrate antiques into spaces that feel fresh, personal, and inviting, and use our heirlooms every day, adding depth and beauty to their patina?

The inspiration for this book is personal. Fifteen years ago, I began to inherit heirlooms—a silver tea service, gilt-rimmed stemware, china, a cut-glass pickle dish, embroidered linens, an antique clock, and countless what-nots, oddments, and bibelots. When I lived in a traditional house in Charleston, South Carolina, it wasn't hard to know what to do with these pieces. They suited the house in terms of age and style, as well as the lifestyle of the city. The same held true when I moved to a mid-nineteenth-century house in New Orleans. Although it was tiny, there was just enough room for bijoux parties glittering with silver and gilt. By the time the trickle of heirlooms turned into a torrent, I was living in a 1930s cottage in the Blue Ridge Mountains—a Hurricane Katrina retreat. There was little room to store anything, much less display it. My inherited china and crystal looked out of place in the dining room, which had a modern floor of tinted concrete, and the living room mantel of salvaged wood refused to be garnished with anything dressier than a pinecone.

A panoply of fine tableware crowded inside my old sideboard, linens languished in the laundry room, and the antique velvet French slipper chairs I bought on a whim were about to acquire ticking slipcovers. I was determined to find creative ways to live comfortably, beautifully, and even practically with all—and I mean all—of these things, so I turned for guidance to friends and colleagues, including collectors, interior designers, style writers, architects, preservationists, and aficionados of old houses and old things. The lessons they shared with me form the substance of this book—an inspirational guide to living with heirlooms and antiques in just about any setting, style, or degree of formality. Some houses are exaggeratedly grand: a 1920s baroque-style villa with a sky-high rotunda in Macon, Georgia, and the late nineteenth-century home of Gilded Age architect Stanford White on Long Island, New York. Others are simple—a cottage in the Blue Ridge Mountains not unlike my own and a primitive Greek Revival plantation house in Alabama. A few are eccentric, including a late-nineteenth-century waterworks and an early twentieth-century fire station, both converted into residences.

The people featured in this book fall into three overlapping categories—the inheritors, the collectors, and the curators. The inheritors are those who don't just receive heirlooms, but choose to cherish them and integrate them into their daily lives. They dine with their silver flatware—and sometimes even put it in the dishwasher. They decorate their mantels and occasional tables with inherited goods. They devise ingenious ways to store and display their heirlooms, keeping them readily at hand or in constant view. Originally, the word heirloom referred to a tool, such as a loom, passed down from one generation to the next. Today, it's most frequently heard in reference to an old-fashioned plant variety that has been revived—heirloom roses, heirloom tomatoes. Both definitions resonate for the inheritors, who put old things to use by using them, reviving lifestyles and memories that might otherwise be lost.

The collectors are another ilk. They are incorrigible acquisitionists who cannot resist the siren call of certain types of objects, whether ancient textiles, eighteenth-century snuffboxes, nineteenth-century landscape paintings, midcentury modern furniture, or stones, bones, feathers, and nests picked up on walks. Nest-builders, they take the things they find and twine them into homes. Sometimes these houses reflect particular tastes—a penchant for early American furniture or obsession with English Midlands pottery. In other cases, they pay homage to a specific place or time, like two houses that celebrate Long Island's heyday of whaling and the China Trade. Sometimes collectors' houses evince dueling passions—French antiques and Anglo-Indian style, midcentury modern furniture and Wedgwood china. Although collectors may choose to live with relics of the past, there's no reason for their homes to feel like shrines or reliquaries. When imagination, wit, and a strong dash of personal taste are added into the mix, the past becomes present and the result is vibrant and inviting.

The third category is the curator, whose special gift was once described to me by a museum director as the art of bringing objects together in poetic conversation. The curators approach to living with heirlooms and antiques is driven less by fascination with family history or a specific type of object than by a talent for combining things in intriguing compositions. The curator has an eye for color and shape and an ear for the stories things tell. They're not afraid to mix things from different periods or countries or to combine the highly crafted with the primitive or nature-made. The compositions they create may serve as three-dimensional travel logs, cataloging their journeys through life with things picked up along the way. Or they may be composed of disparate objects selected by someone who simply likes what he likes and doesn't feel the need to explain. Curators let things do the talking, because they trust them to speak to the heart and senses.

In speaking about heirlooms and antiques, a certain amount of reverence and poetry is hard to avoid. They are elemental objects compounded of earth, water, air, and fire. They are human, in that they would not exist without the spark of imagination and touch of the human hand. As tangible mementoes of people, places, and events that may no longer exist, they are almost immortal. They are silent storytellers, recounting narratives we know by heart as well as mysteries we will never fathom. But they are also simply things—things we like or don't like, things we know what to do with, things we don't know what to do with, and things we don't want to do without. There are no rules about living with them except to take what's old and keep it young by making it a part of daily life. Loom-like, heirlooms and antiques have the power to weave the past with the present—as long as they are put to use.

PREVIOUS SPREAD: *For a luncheon party, Charleston artist Marty Whaley Adams combined heirloom tableware and linens with Mexican stemware and crystal candlesticks.*

OPPOSITE: *A pass-through butler's pantry allows architect Norman Askins and his wife, Joane, to enjoy objects they rarely use, including a nineteenth-century English cruet set, Canton, Delft, and creamware plates, and a marble-and-zinc Italian scale.*

A Menagerie of Things

We inherit and acquire a multiplicity of objects, but often wonder how to integrate them into our lives. The answer is not to treat them as precious relics, but rather to bring them into daily life. Set the table with heirloom flatware and china, repurpose vessels and linens creatively, garnish tabletops, mantels, and walls with abandon, and display even the humblest object in full view. When the past is present, the opportunities are boundless.

GARNISH THE HOUSE

Antique textiles, architectural fragments, decanters, highly decorative furnishings, books, boxes, and bibelots add texture, color, and often a touch of quirk to interiors. Load up a room with things you own but don't know what to do with—then pare a bit, or don't. The result will be an engaging interior that arouses the senses and piques curiosity.

SET THE TABLE

Treat yourself and your guests by using sterling silver, antique china, embroidered linens, hand-carved horn, and brilliant cut glass on a regular basis. Entirely antique place settings are exquisite, but combinations of traditional and contemporary design are equally engaging. If you never set the same table twice, you will find that you use everything you own, from the exalted silver punch bowl to the humble crystal saltcellar.

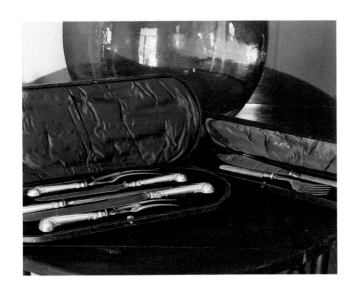

RE-ENVISION ANTIQUES

Why should a pitcher be used exclusively as a vessel for water? Why should a piece of antique embroidery or a family quilt packed with mothballs in a chest? If you inherit traditional furniture, but live in a modern environment, don't give it away. If you toss out preconceptions, and look at each object anew, the opportunities to recycle, renew, and reuse are boundless.

KEEP THINGS IN SIGHT

Whether you employ something daily and want to keep it handy or simply love to look at it, there are endless ways to store and display antiques and heirlooms in plain view. Glass-fronted cabinets, open shelving, butler's tables, and wall displays are just a few options that allow antiques and heirlooms to shine.

Antique Meets Modern

There's nothing new about the idea of antique meets modern. Much of what has been considered modern—even trendy—has roots in the past. The ever-popular klismos chair is inspired by ancient Greek art and venerable Chinese designs have long informed the shapes and finish of furniture and decorative objects. Whether they are old or new, things that are beautiful can coexist in harmony. Tastemakers have recognized this for centuries, recycling elements from the antique world into chic interiors like Josephine Bonaparte's Pompeii-influenced dining room at Chateau de Malmaison. Renowned decorators from the Adam brothers to Syrie Maugham were not afraid to intersperse contemporary objects with antiques. This is because they recognized the vast potential of combining the old and the new. In some cases, antique and modern objects can comingle quietly in understated style. In bolder combinations, a kind of combustion occurs, allowing each individual object to be seen in a bright new light.

Interiors where the old meets the new testify to the discriminating eye of their creators—iconoclastic individuals who are uninhibited by the rules of time. Why not put a pair of eighteenth-century Venetian candelabra on a 1980s Joseph D'Urso Racetrack table or hang a Jasper Johns screen print of an American flag above a Victorian mantel? Who's to say that Danish modern furniture and French art deco chairs might not work in a nineteenth-century New England farmhouse? The houses illustrated in the following pages represent a spirit of creative anachronism that keeps style alive and remind us how beautifully and provocatively the past can intersect the present in everyday life.

Old Made New

When Mary Catherine Crowe moved from her Tudor-style house in Birmingham, Alabama, to a Federal Revival house in another neighborhood, she was ready for a change. "I loved the old house and enjoyed furnishing it with English and French antiques, but everything was dark, especially the library, which was painted a shade called Mulled Wine," she recalls. In the new house, she saw the potential to create an entirely different environment. Nearly everything, from the antiquated wiring to the rotted floors and window frames, required attention, but Crowe saw this as an invitation to refresh and reinterpret the house. Removing all but two of the interior doors and enlarging openings on the ground floor changed the character of the house instantly. Once the traditional multi-paned windows were replaced with taller, steel-framed ones and the walls were painted white, the transformation was complete.

"When the doors were gone, the whole place appeared open and contemporary," she notes. "I love the experience of seeing through the house."

These changes also reframed Crowe's collection of art and antiques. "I honestly think my things look better here because the light is so beautiful and the white walls show off their lines," she observes. Illustrating her point, a pair of English campaign chairs with curved, intersecting slats creates a dramatic silhouette against the pale walls of the front hall. These, along with a table fashioned from the roots and stump of a tree, become the art in the room. In the living room, where a minimalist limestone mantel replaced the original neoclassical example, antiques that might be overlooked in a traditional house take on new life. Brushed by light spilling in through the windows, the hand-carved walnut of a two-hundred-year old French *court de buffet* enlivens a corner of the room. While the

boldly curved legs of a late nineteenth-century *lit de repos* are eye-catching, Crowe chose the piece for the way it framed the view to the terrace beyond the window. The same train of thought led to the selection of the pair of 1950s Lucite chairs standing nearby. "I love the idea of furniture that I can see through," she comments.

The delicate tracery of the Hepplewhite-style dining chairs offers a similarly transparent effect. With a pale finish that lends an almost modern air, the decorative chairs become understated, allowing the books lining the room to become the primary focus. While her architect envisioned a space with paneling and drapery, Crowe opted for curtain-less windows and floor-to-ceiling bookshelves that showcase leather-bound volumes published by her late husband, Les Adams. "It's important for people to know that they can take an old house and bring it up to date—and that the same thing can happen with antiques," says Crowe.

The master bedroom offers in master class in old-made-new. During the remodeling, small windows were replaced with taller, steel-frame ones with multiple panes that temper their modern scale. New upholstery, including white linen on a French chair and ottoman, leopard print on a French painted bench, and chartreuse linen on an Empire-style bergere, imparts a fresh look to familiar pieces. Linen draperies filter light without distracting from the room's simplicity. Previously disguised by hangings, a steel bed with modern lines is another transplant from the Tudor house. Now stripped down to its minimalist frame, the bed makes a strong contemporary statement, throwing the dark wood and strong lines of the antiques into dramatic relief. "When you combine things from several different periods," says Crowe, "everything comes to life."

OPPOSITE: *In the center hall, a contemporary front door is juxtaposed with original oak floorboards. "Old oak floors have an ambiance that's hard to reproduce," Crowe observes. "They carry the soul of a house in their grain."*

PRECEDING SPREAD: *The living room is decorated in shades of white and sand. Tall steel-framed windows and a contemporary mantel provide a minimalist backdrop for antiques that include an English Jacobean-style chair, a baroque mirror finished with gesso, and an ecclesiastical candle stand.*

ABOVE AND OPPOSITE: *In the dining room, the burnished colors of gilded leather bindings offer a warmer and richer effect than traditional paneling. An antique English library table is a perfect choice for the book-lined room, where Hepplewhite-style chairs and an Italian giltwood chandelier add more formal notes.*

ABOVE LEFT: *With industrial metal bookshelves and a chrome and leather chair drawn up to a hand-carved Italian table, the study demonstrates Crowe's theory that combining different periods and materials gives everything a fresher look.*

ABOVE: *A portrait of sisters painted in 1947 by Howard Chandler Christie, who also painted the murals of New York's Café des Artistes, reminds Crowe of the many happy hours she spent there before the restaurant closed.*

ABOVE: *Crowe retained much of the bedroom furniture from her Tudor-style house. There, the steel four-poster bed was heavily draped. Now, with the spare frame exposed, it provides a contemporary focal point, balancing the formality of French and English antiques.*

Mother Knows Best

When David Feld, former editor of major shelter magazines, and his partner, Kurt Purdy, returned from the East Coast to their hometown of Dallas, decorating help came from an unexpected source. "I enlisted the person whose advice I had pretty much ignored my whole life," says Feld.

"It's natural to rebel against your mother, but after a certain amount of time, you realize that sometimes mother really does know best."

Although Feld's childhood home was traditional in style, when his parents acquired a New York apartment in the 1980s, his mother, Anne, embraced modernism. "The apartment was decorated with archly modern furniture from Knoll, mixed in with old English pine and kilim rugs, and the effect was smashing," Feld recalls.

During their house hunt, Feld and Purdy briefly succumbed to the charms of the quainter cottages of Dallas's Park Cities, but ultimately, they chose a simply detailed 1940s house. While the two undertook the move, Anne Feld served as general contractor. When the furniture came, she placed it, choosing two leather Joseph D'Urso sofas and a Mies van der Rohe Barcelona table for the rear sitting room. Once Feld arrived, he mixed in an eighteenth-century gilded Italian mirror and a contemporary "fauxbusson" carpet to provide a counterpoint to the modern pieces. He also added two vividly colored floral photographic prints by Marc Quinn, which he describes as "the chintz in the room." Avid collectors of china, porcelain, and pottery, the residents chose a small selection of Wedgwood creamware and drabware to display on the mantel. "We have a porcelain problem," admits Purdy, who stores most of their collection in custom-designed shelving in the garage.

More prize pieces are displayed in the front living room, including three seventeenth-century Ming bowls recovered from the hold of a wrecked Asian cargo ship. Crystal candlesticks and a pair of cased opaline vases decorated with cherry blossoms contribute to the traditional aspect of the room. In one corner, Paul Frankl Neckline chairs add a midcentury touch to an octagonal Regency-style table. Feld, who discovered the chairs in a garage sale just a few blocks away while still in his twenties, replaced their orange flame-stitch upholstery with striped Travers velvet broadcloth that accentuates their V-shaped silhouette.

The most dramatic intersection of antique and modern styles occurs in the dining room, where a granite-topped Racetrack table, designed in 1985 by D'Urso for Knoll, stands beneath a simple bronze d'oré chandelier. Six Mies Brno chairs purchased for Feld's father's New York conference room surround the table. With their original blue upholstery replaced by velvet with an antique napped texture and golden tone, the chrome-framed chairs assume a softer attitude. A gilded mirror reflects this composition of charcoal, chrome, and gold. With original glass and an unusual motif featuring a palette and architectural tools, the eighteenth-century piece is one of Feld's favorites. "I stalked it for fifteen years before finally getting it," he says.

Other pieces in the room came more easily, including eighteenth-century Venetian candelabra—a present from Feld's parents—and his grandmother's gilt-rimmed champagne and water glasses. A setting for thirty-six of platinum-resist lusterware designed for Wedgwood was literally delivered to his front door, a gift from a friend who died soon after. "I don't like to sentimentalize objects, but each of these things means something to us," says Feld. "We've pared back, surrounding ourselves only with things that have happy associations or that we just like to look at—because at the end of the day, you want to come home to a pretty room."

OPPOSITE: *Neckline chairs by American midcentury modernist Paul Frankl are surprisingly compatible with the nineteenth-century porcelain on the Regency-style table.*

ABOVE: *The library furnishings are limited to three major pieces: a Mies van der Rohe Barcelona table and a pair of Joseph D'Urso sofas produced by Knoll in the 1980s. A floral carpet reminiscent of Aubusson and Axminster designs and an eighteenth-century Italian mirror contrast with the sleek lines of the modern pieces. Vibrant photographs by Marc Quinn energize the neutral setting.*

OPPOSITE: *A narrow bookcase provides a perfect place to display pieces from Purdy's collection of Wedgwood jasperware, including pairs of bough pots, cylindrical enamelware spill vases with a peony motif, and urns, among them a piece of rare tricolor jasperware. The pristine elegance of tiny Wedgwood buttons contrasts with the irregular green patina of a Buddha's head, found in a shop on Christopher Street in New York.*

PRECEDING SPREAD: *Chairs based on a 1930s design by Jean-Michel Frank and covered in Summerhill linen offer a clean, classic look in the front living room. French opaline lamps with a Greek key motif forge a connection with the Piranesi etching of ancient Rome hanging above a lacquered 1920s Jansen console.*

OPPOSITE AND ABOVE: *The restrained architecture and pewter-colored walls of the dining room provide a quiet backdrop for a dynamic combination of old and new. The trumeau mirror, once part of an eighteenth-century French room, makes a dramatic statement, balanced by the strength of the 1980s Racetrack table designed by Joseph D'Urso and 1934 Mies Brno chairs.*

Table settings are placed directly on the dark granite surface for a more contemporary effect. Feld creates a striking silver and white composition by combining platinum-resist Wedgwood lusterware with silver flatware, including eighteenth-century Scottish shell and a pattern designed by Elsa Peretti for Tiffany, and his great-grandmother's crocheted lace napkins.

Strength and Simplicity

Unlike many Victorian houses, where ponderous architectural details pose serious competition to everything else in the rooms, this 1880 San Antonio dwelling offers a relatively clean, if not exactly blank, slate. According to Chris Carson, the architect who directed its restoration in 1981, this restraint resulted from the collaboration between the original, English-born architect Alfred Giles and his client, German-born banker Carl Groos.

"The design started out much more typically Victorian," says Carson, "but Groos wanted the house to be simple and strong."

With its filigreed cast-iron porch layered over a flat plane of Texas limestone, embellished only by beveled quoins, the facade demonstrates the success with which their visions merged. This same harmony of opposites is found within, where uncomplicated moldings are the rule and highly decorative details, like frothy cornices and gilded gasoliers, are the exception.

Because the ceilings are high, the walls wide, and windows large and plentiful, the house easily absorbs its most ornamental elements, leaving plenty of breathing space for furniture and art. This is the aspect of the dwelling that appealed most to the current owner, a collector whose acquisitions range from nineteenth-century Luminist marine scenes to twentieth-century abstract prints by Jasper Johns and Donald Judd. His collection also includes English, American, and European furniture from the seventeenth to the twentieth centuries, and hundreds of books on subjects as diverse as sailing in the tropics to Texas Hill Country history. The house accommodates these varied possessions as easily as its most dramatic architectural feature, a show-stopping staircase with massive gothic newel posts that would easily break the stylometer in a gaudier Victorian house.

The owner chose to display a series of minimalist prints by Donald Judd on the walls surrounding the staircase. These serene compositions of blue and white rectangles seem to float, balancing the weightiness of the stairs. Their cool, uniform palette allows the natural tones of the hall, including a parquet floor with alternating boards of oak and darker pecan, to appear richer and warmer by contrast. A more varied representation of the collection is displayed in the adjoining double parlor, where works range from a fifteenth-century Netherlandish portrait to a contemporary resin and fiberglass sculpture by John McCracken. While the back parlor contains vernacular American antiques, the front parlor's sole piece of furniture, other than a Steinway grand piano, is a Barcelona couch designed in 1929 by Mies van der Rohe. It's hard to imagine such disparate things sharing space congenially—especially when that space has ornate moldings and ceiling medallions—but they do.

"I love combining things from different eras and styles," the collector explains. "I've always been interested in having at least one modern piece of furniture or contemporary painting in each room, so the house doesn't look like a museum." Throughout the house, off-white walls, curtain-less windows, and wood floors with faded oriental carpets provide an understated backdrop for animated juxtapositions of art and architecture. One of the most striking can be found in the library, where a red-white-and-blue flag print by Jasper Johns floats above a massive black-slate mantelpiece. In addition to books, the room also contains eighteenth-century Windsor chairs and a charcoal drawing by Philip Guston. "The owner has an eye for finding the right piece and placing it carefully," says Carson. "What makes it all work is that the background is light and the architecture doesn't compete with the art."

OPPOSITE: A seascape by Luminist painter Fitz Henry Lane is prized by the owner, a lifelong sailor and a collector of maritime scenes. The simple lines and worn blue paint of a rustic nineteenth-century mule chest complement the colors and composition of the painting.

OPPOSITE: *Strong color and pure geometry hold their own against high Victorian detail in the double parlor, where lithographs from Josef Albers's "Homage to the Square" series share a corner with painted wood cubes discovered in an antiques shop.*

ABOVE: *The bold precision of neoclassical door surrounds, carved from Texas longleaf pine, becomes a sculptural element in the wide center hall, which is hung with artwork by Jasper Johns, Christo, and Donald Judd. The door surrounds also frame views of the art in the adjacent spaces, including a vivid resin-and-fiberglass piece by John McCracken.*

OPPOSITE: *Although the moldings and gasolier in the front parlor are elaborate, they hover high above the floor, leaving plenty of space for a more minimalist expression below. The leather-and-steel Barcelona chaise, designed by Mies van der Rohe in 1929, has become a modernist icon. A linear abstract painting by Burgoyne Diller from 1930 completes the vignette.*

ABOVE: *While the Italo-Iberian baroque walnut table echoes the weighty boldness of the central staircase, large works on paper including a mixed media piece by Christo and a monotype by Jasper Johns appear to float on the tall white walls of the entrance hall.*

ABOVE LEFT: *A similar mantel in the front parlor holds a fifteenth-century Netherlandish portrait above which an untitled 1981 silkscreen by Jasper Johns is mounted*

OVERLEAF: *Towering banks of bookcases are easily accommodated in the library, where a trestle table is piled high with favorite volumes. In front, eighteenth-century Windsor chairs flank a table of glass and chrome, and a Philip Guston drawing stands in the window behind.*

OPPOSITE: *The primary colors and graphic lines of a silkscreen from Jasper Johns's Flag series add graphic energy to the space above the massive mantel in the library. The flat geometry of the composition contrasts with the shadowy self-portrait by nineteenth-century American artist Edward H. Barnard to the left.*

Connecticut Collage

The bucolic hamlet of Cornwall, Connecticut, has long offered a pair of New York professionals and their children respite from the intensity of urban living. For years, the family rented an early nineteenth-century farmhouse possessed of great charm, as well as a menagerie of dilapidated antique and vintage furniture. According to the former renters, the family owning the house kept it as a relic, resisting change to anything, including sofas with drooping springs and floors with sagging joists. When the house became available for sale, the couple purchased it and began a process of respectful restoration, retaining as much original material as possible while also expanding it with a contemporary barn-like addition. During the disposition of its contents, the new owners bought the farm-style table where they had shared meals for years—now a centerpiece of the new kitchen. With layers of family heirlooms and antiques and vintage pieces collected in New England and France, the rest of house's contents reflects the personal histories of its occupants.

One of the owners grew up in Paris, frequently returning to the States for sojourns at an early eighteenth-century family home in Boston that was furnished with a mix of formal and eccentric antiques.

"My mother was from Virginia and my father was a mad collector of everything," she recalls.

Her husband grew up in New York City, grandson of a Jewish family who fled Italy during World War II and prospered in New York. In the 1950s and 1960s, his parents furnished their home entirely in Danish modern style, included the dining table and chairs now in the Connecticut dining room. After marrying, the couple lived in France for five years where frequent expeditions to flea markets in Paris, Provence, and elsewhere yielded a collection of antique and vintage

textiles, art deco chairs, and other objects now installed in their American farmhouse.

The successful integration of such diverse pieces posed a challenge. Commissioning interior designer Fawn Galli to direct the decoration and architect Douglas Wright to restore and update the house, they assembled a creative team to fulfill their vision. "We integrated contemporary wallpapers, fabrics, and furniture with and rummage sale finds and inherited pieces to create a farmhouse look with a bit of a twist," says Galli. Thinking creatively about the past and the present, Wright enlarged the house with an addition that resembles regional barns but enters the realm of modernism with black exterior siding and folding glass doors. He integrated materials salvaged from the original farmhouse in arresting ways, as in a hallway floored with boards painted a variety of colors by previous residents. "The effect is like a collage or an oriental carpet," Wright explains.

Throughout the house, elements from the past and present come together in collage-like juxtapositions. In several rooms, Fawn integrated contemporary wallpapers, fabrics, and furniture with older pieces to create a fresh, layered look. Antique French bed sheets were recycled as curtains and cowhide splattered with black paint—an homage to Jackson Pollack—upholstered the Danish modern chairs. In the kitchen, original hand-hewn support beams, stainless steel appliances, cabinets designed in vintage style, French art deco chairs, and pillows made from French rice sacks combine to create an atmosphere that is as chic as it is relaxed. The end result is a house where the past meets the present and the European intersects with the American with effortless grace and charm.

OPPOSITE: *Spatterware bowls and vivid sunflowers complement the palette of primary colors.*

OPPOSITE AND ABOVE: *With a pressed-tin ceiling in a simple geometric pattern, hand-hewn beams, a contemporary cast-iron wood-stove, and French art deco chairs, the kitchen designed by Wright is simultaneously traditional and modern. Pillows covered in vintage French textiles and an antique American flag combine on the banquette for an international expression.*

OPPOSITE AND ABOVE: *The dining room combines rustic pine-plank flooring and sleek plate glass doors with steel frames that fold open to reveal the surrounding landscape. Reminiscent of Shaker simplicity, the lines of a midcentury Danish table and chairs complement the rural New England setting. Black paint spattered on white hide seats adds an unexpected, contemporary detail.*

ABOVE: *The second floor of the farmhouse was reconfigured to create a combined stair hall and library accommodating a large book collection. Figured wallpaper reminiscent of vintage British floral patterns adds graphic energy to the space as does a patchwork pattern of colors on the floor — vestiges of original paint colors employed by previous residents.*

OPPOSITE: *A screened porch runs the length of the farmhouse, opening to views of the Litchfield Hills. Surrounded by director's chairs, a simple table found in a nearby antiques shop offers a perfect setting for outdoor meals.*

Photographs by Costa Picadas

Living Color

There is a common misconception that decorating with antiques and heirlooms is a serious endeavor requiring a neutral palette and an attitude of stiff formality. In truth, the rooms of the past were vividly colored. We can travel back in time to ancient Egypt or Pompeii and Herculaneum for reminders that brilliant color provided the setting for decorative objects that have inspired artists and craftsmen for centuries. In Georgian England, vermillion was a favorite choice of wall color, not only because it was eye-catching, but also because it was expensive—indicating the owner's exalted social status. Vivid shades of yellow and green were favored in Williamsburg, Virginia. Dulled over time, the colonial city's walls suggested that early Americans preferred muted tones, but later conservation efforts revealed the daring tastes of the era. Regency gold and Adam blue also illustrate the fact that previous generations were far from color shy.

The houses that follow demonstrate that daring, unexpected color choices are highly effective when decorating with antiques and heirlooms. So-called "brown furniture" glows against a cerulean backdrop. Pale French and Swedish antiques come to life in a lavender room. And gilt looks good when paired with just about any intense hue. Following the lead of the talented colorists featured here, it's easy to recast antique furniture and decorative objects as star characters in dramatic scenes.

Jewel Box

Ringed by high hedges and gardens, this neoclassical residence in Dallas is first glimpsed from a pleached-oak allée that evokes the romantic approaches to French manor houses. With elegance, drama, glamour, and restraint, the house is a perfect reflection of its owner, a leading figure in Texas civic life. After living for thirty years in a modernist house with maximal glass and minimalist detail, the owner was ready for a change.

"I wanted something classical and European, but not with a lot of carving and gold," she says.

Dallas-born, Los Angeles-based architect Richardson Robertson III understood completely, delivering plans for a limestone pavilion with exquisite materials, understated classical details, and spacious, light-filled rooms.

The refined architecture of the rooms provides an ideal setting for the client's collection of English, European, and Chinese antiques, many of which came from her modernist home. The understated quality of detail also issued an open invitation to interior designer Beverly Field to combine the antiques with a selection of ultra contemporary objects and to introduce a sophisticated color palette. This approach finds full expression in the grand salon, where a monumental rococo mirror and an assortment of eighteenth- and nineteenth-century Continental chairs combine with cone-shaped chairs by Verner Panton and contemporary shagreen-covered tables. "The contemporary furniture moves everything forward and keeps things interesting," says Field. The collector agrees, "When you combine the antique with the modern, it's the best of both worlds."

Field brought her skills as a colorist to the project, employing a spectrum of shades ranging from lipstick red to iceberg green to create rooms with just as wide a spectrum of moods. In the groin-vaulted gallery, the pale tones of hand-finished plaster and marble parquet suggested a palette of ivory, gray, and silver, with color provided only by blue-and-white Chinese jars. Blue tones find fuller expression in the sitting area that serves as an antechamber to the grand salon. With a banquette upholstered in silvery-blue Fortuny silk, pillows in deeper shades of blue—two re-fashioned from an art deco gown—and Italian chairs with pale blue-gray seats and turquoise backs, the intimate space provides a moment of serenity before guests enter into the exuberance of the larger space. "I like to live in a place that feels serene, but that also has vibrant color," the owner says. "Bright colors cheer you up and cheer your guests, too." It would certainly take a glum guest to resist the appeal of the pink swivel chairs and cerulean pillows embroidered with dragonflies.

While the grand salon is extroverted and the deep-red library, warm and inviting, the master bedroom is purely magical. "Anyone waking up in that room would feel like a princess," says Brad Kelly, an architectural project manager and the owner's nephew, who made sure all his aunt's dreams came true. De Gournay wallpaper, with birds and flowers arrayed on a sky-blue ground, and a Venetian chandelier in similar hues set a dreamy tone. "I tried to capture the color of the sky at the peak of day," explains Field, who also introduced shades of pink and green and occasional touches of gilt. Although more muted in hue, color also plays a role in the dining room, where pale celadon paneling offers a backdrop for a collection of fine Chinese exportware, and in the morning room, where ice-blue walls temper the bright Texas light. "The house is perfect expression of my aunt," Kelly observes. "There is no drabness to her personality or to the house. It is a jewel box, and she is the jewel."

OPPOSITE: *In the entrance gallery, hints of color, including the blue of antique Chinese jars and pink glass petals of early twentieth-century French sconces, enliven a serene palette of ivory and gray.*

ABOVE: *In the grand salon, contemporary art and furniture, including swivel chairs by Verner Panton and contemporary drawings by Dallas artist Otis Jones, combine with antiques. Gilded columns from India and a massive rococo mirror add high-style details that contrast with the smaller scale and simpler silhouettes of chairs and sofas. Fuchsia cone chairs and the turquoise backing of gilded Italian chairs invigorate the room with shots of strong color.*

ABOVE LEFT: *In the bedroom, luminous shades of blue combine with pink and violet to create a garden of delight. French and Italian antiques with painted, gilded, and polished wood finishes work in concert against a patterned field of hand-painted de Gournay wallpaper.*

LEFT: *A Venetian chandelier with floral pendants completes the petal-strewn garden fantasy.*

ABOVE: *Glacier blue paint and a glass-topped Italian table create a cool, serene atmosphere in the morning room. Thanks to their curved silhouette, contemporary leather-and-chrome swivel chairs combine surprisingly easily with eighteenth-century Swedish chairs.*

LEFT: *Centered around a Georgian English mirror, eighteenth-century Chinese plates purchased in London cover the dining room walls in a dynamic arrangement that balances a variety of colors, patterns, sizes, and shapes.*

ABOVE: *Like the grand salon to which it leads, this sitting area combines traditional and modern sensibilities. The pale floor, bright-white paneled walls, antique and modern furnishings, and elegant blue-and-white palette make the space both sophisticated and inviting.*

Gilt-y Pleasures

Some people like to go outside to play, but Quinn Peeper and Michael Harold prefer to stay inside in a place they call "The Great Indoors." Whether touring houses abroad or remaining at home in New Orleans, Louisiana, they find their greatest pleasures within four walls. Peeper, born in Arkansas and reared in Memphis, Tennessee, elected to complete his medical training at Oxford University because, he says, "I loved English country houses and wanted to be nearer to them." Harold, a native of New Orleans and Francophile from the crib, became an Anglophile as well, thanks in part to his partner's fascination. The pair's love affair with the English country house reached new heights when several years ago, their friend Lady Henrietta Spencer-Churchill suggested they wed at Blenheim Palace, the family seat of her father, the Duke of Marlborough.

When Peeper and Harold purchased a Greek Revival house in New Orleans a year later, they integrated the design lessons they learned abroad. A pair of parlors, graced with thirteen-foot-high ceilings, marble mantels, and handsome moldings, reminded them of rooms across the Atlantic. They transformed one parlor into a music room with a grand piano, Louis XVI chairs (a favorite style of Chopin), and sconces that once belonged to acclaimed conductor Arturo Toscanini. For the walls, they chose muted green paint to accentuate the tones of richly grained walnut furniture, saffron damask, and displays of books and porcelain. The second parlor, which they prefer to call the "great room," is an homage to the libraries of Holkham Hall, a Palladian style country house in Norfolk, England. Scaled-down versions of Holkham's library cases, originally designed by eighteenth-century English architect William Kent, line one wall of the room. Finished with ivory paint and gilt trim, the neoclassical cases cast the richly colored spines of the collection of rare books into high relief.

OPPOSITE: The library secretary bookcase displays prized books, a crystal and bronze-d'oré standish, and an eighteenth-century Chinese Export cup and saucer.

Among the volumes are a gilt-embossed first edition of the first biography of Queen Elizabeth I, published in 1630, and an 1882 edition of *Alice in Wonderland* with a red leather spine detailed with gilt characters from the narrative. The cases also display colorful curiosities and souvenirs of travel, including Old Paris porcelain urns, precious red coral, and a bronze bust of the Duke of Wellington mounted on a bluejohn base. "We are like kids who have to buy a prize wherever we go," admits Quinn, who recently purchased a collection of multi-colored beaded circumcision caps in the souks of Istanbul. These are displayed in a George III secretary bookcase in the room next door, a cozy library upholstered in golden beige corduroy. The fabric is trimmed in scarlet passementerie and accented by a contemporary red Kuba rug, creating a warm atmosphere where both books and bibelots are shown to advantage.

"There's nothing like a bit of gilt to elevate a space."

For the walls of a spacious dining room formed by joining two smaller rooms, the residents chose a chalky shade of terra-cotta that complements Pompeian-style panels inspired by those in Marie Antoinette's private chambers at Fontainebleau. The muted gleam of a gilded Directoire mirror and Swedish bronze-d'oré chandelier add the burnished glow of gold to the room. While the dining room furnishings are primarily French, table settings are usually more eclectic, combining Continental European, English, and American silver, crystal, and porcelain. Choosing from a collection that includes an Old Paris service with apricot and gold designs and eighteenth-century Blind Earl porcelain with a raised pattern of green leaves and vividly hued flowers, Peeper uses different patterns for each course. Guests are surrounded by beauty no matter where they are in the house, even in the small hallway leading to the powder room, where gilt filets and a gilded Louis XVI style console add unexpected glamour.

OPPOSITE AND ABOVE: *Painted a soft shade of taupe, the hall is animated by gilt, including gold-leaf fillets at the cornice and an elaborately carved Louis XVI mirror and console. At the music room end, a plaster ram's head once belonging to designer Albert Hadley presides over framed invitations to musical evenings hosted by Italian composer and violinist Felice Giardini, eighteenth-century conductor and director of the Italian Opera in London. Below, a "rafraichissoire" holds a champagne cooler, William Yeoward flutes, and Murano dessert-wine glasses.*

LEFT AND ABOVE: *High ceilings, marble mantels, and handsome ceiling medallions inspired Peeper and Harold to evoke an English country house atmosphere. Bookcases in the drawing room reference those at Holkham Hall and at Goodwood House. The book collection features fine bindings by Zaehnsdorf, Riviere, Bickers, and Sangorski and Sutcliffe. Blue and red coral and a miniature bronze bust of the Duke of Wellington on a Blue John stand add shape and texture to the shelves while echoing the colors of the surrounding bindings.*

ABOVE: *A pale but vibrant amethyst provides the ideal backdrop for the painted bedroom furniture, which includes a pair of English Regency chairs and a Directoire "secrétaire à abattant" that opens to reveal a dramatic burnt-umber interior. A leopard-skin pattern carpet adds a touch of Madeleine Castaing glamour to the room.*

OPPOSITE: *Wall coverings of golden beige corduroy contribute texture and warmth to an intimate sitting room. Furniture includes a George III secretary bookcase filled with a complete collection of P. G. Wodehouse novels and an 1860 painted ballroom chair from Windsor Castle. A Louis XVI armchair upholstered in terra-cotta leather and a nineteenth-century salesman's model of a canon, refashioned as a table, are among the few French pieces that have slipped into this very English room.*

ABOVE: *A large collection of antique tableware includes plates in the Blind Earl pattern, made for the Fifth Earl of Coventry after he was blinded in a hunting accident. Peeper describes the raised foliate decoration as "porcelain Braille."*

RIGHT: *The chalky terra-cotta wall color was inspired by the dining room at Chateau de Malmaison, decorated in the Pompeïan style in the early nineteenth century at the request of Empress Josephine. The gold and apricot borders of an Old Paris service perfectly complement the color scheme. Wall panels painted with classical motifs, after Marie Antoinette's boudoir in Versailles, fluted columns, and a Directoire mirror with a medallion depicting a Greek god extend the allusion to the ancient world.*

Artful Compositions

With coral-colored clapboard walls, green shutters, and creamy trim, Joe and Evelyn Adams' 1854 cottage in Macon, Georgia, stands out amid the white-columned houses surrounding it. An unconventional approach to traditional style is equally evident in the rooms inside, where portraits rub shoulders with abstract paintings and a seventeenth-century Brussels tapestry shares space with a 1960s Fornasetti leopard rug. "We are adventurous collectors," says Evelyn. "Wherever we go, we discover things that speak to us— then we have to find a place for them." According to her husband, an artist, the trick to combining objects success-fully is composing them with the same attention to color, texture, and form he brings to painting. "I move things constantly, trying pieces out in different places until the composition feels right," explains Joe.

While the white-painted Greek Revival-style moldings and paneling are traditional, dark gray walls appear more modern, making both new and antique furniture seem at home. The paint color was inspired by a contemporary sofa upholstered in charcoal-gray leather that Joe paired with a zebra skin rug in similar tones. A crimson French chinoiserie commode stands in one corner beneath a gilt-and-grisaille panel reputedly salvaged from Paris Singer's Palm Beach estate. These two pieces contribute bright color and sheen to the otherwise neutral room. Into this mix, Adams added a Lucite table. "It seemed like a good idea to use a piece of furniture that would disappear," he observes.

A vignette in the narrow center hall also demonstrates the painter's skill at arranging three-dimensional compo-sitions. As in the parlor, dark grayish-brown walls with white trim set off high-impact objects, including a large painted screen depicting Napoleon's African campaign. Black-painted furniture stands beneath it, including a pair of saber-leg chairs and a Chinese altar table, garnished with clusters of white coral, a plaster bust, and Old Paris porcelain. These contribute highlights and texture, but the 1960s scarlet Fornasetti rug with a leopard skin motif is what truly brings the vignette to life, introducing a bold splash of color and an exotic motif.

In the cream-colored dining room across the hall, staples of eighteenth- and nineteenth-century Southern hospitality, including blue-and-white Willowware, Famille Rose china, and English silver serving pieces, form a tableau atop a Maryland Federal sideboard. A portrait of a pearl-bedecked lady in an ornate frame hangs above it. Across the room, one of Joe's brightly colored canvases surmounts a carved marble mantel. "There isn't any reason not to introduce a strong modern painting into a traditional setting," the artist points out.

"You simply have to make sure that every-thing has room to breathe. Color choice has a lot to do with that."

The Adamses employed a similar strategy in the small guestroom, where a serene shade of blue easily absorbs decorative objects, including a collection of polychrome porcelain decanters depicting Napoleon and his generals, mounted high on the wall with ornate gilded brackets. "It's our grandson's room when he visits, so we wanted to include something interesting to look at but well out of reach," Evelyn comments. In the kitchen, built in 1870 and remodeled several times, off-white paint covers plank walls, drawing attention to the rugged brick of the original fireplace and grain of the reclaimed Georgia pine floor and ceiling boards. With so much natural color and texture in the space, there seemed little sense in adding strong decorations. Instead, the couple chose simple arrangements of blue-and-white china platters, baskets, mounted antlers, framed silhouettes, and a nineteenth-century portrait of a country maiden. "When it comes to adding color, texture, and antiques, no room is too small or utilitarian," Joe declares.

OPPOSITE: *Colorful glazes on a group of Chinese figures reflect the vivid hues of an abstract painting by Joe Adams, which hangs over a Renaissance Revival mantel in the dining room.*

OPPOSITE: *Charcoal-brown walls, a twentieth-century Lucite table, and a contemporary leather sofa bring the second parlor into the modern age, while Roman shades with Greek Key trim and a fluted column proffer neoclassical details. A Florentine commode with vermilion paint and ormolu pulls and a pair of gilt and grisaille panels, reputedly from the Palm Beach estate of Paris Singer, add high-style drama to the mix.*

ABOVE: *Offering a striking study in black and white, ebonized Empire-style chairs and a Chinese altar table combine with Old Paris porcelain, a plaster bust, and clusters of coral. A vibrantly painted screen depicting Napoleon's Egyptian campaign and a Fornasetti carpet add color and pattern to the arrangement.*

OPPOSITE AND ABOVE: *Painted pine plank walls and a ceiling of wood salvaged from a Georgia farmhouse create an appropriate setting for the original brick chimney and pine mantelpiece in the kitchen. While baskets, stoneware crocks, and Willowware serving pieces are typical of old Southern kitchens, the molded resin bear is a bit more fanciful. Facing the hearth is a small sofa covered in mattress ticking and surrounded by pieces collected over the years—silhouettes from the famous Brimfield antiques show in Massachusetts, blue rimmed platters, and a painting of a young girl collecting eggs, discovered at a Macon estate sale.*

OPPOSITE AND ABOVE: *The guest room has a Napoleonic theme with prints of eighteenth-century personages and porcelain decanters depicting Napoleon's generals. Mounted on the wall with gilded eagle brackets, the decanters add bright color and a fanciful touch to the room.*

French Chic

Paris-born interior designer Florence de Dampierre seems to have that extra gene Parisians possess—the chic gene. Listed in *W* magazine as one of the best-dressed women in the world, she also excels at dressing rooms that are eye-catching and elegant. "Basically, my approach is to decorate appropriately for the kind of life that takes place in a room," de Dampierre explains.

"Then I like to mix high with low, sophistication with whimsy."

One of the best places to observe a designer's aesthetic is in his or her own home, and this is the case with Florence. While her approach is evident throughout the Greek Revival house she shares with her husband, Sean Mathis, and their daughter, Valentina, in Litchfield, Connecticut, it is most fully expressed in newest additions to the property—a garden room and a pool pavilion.

When the family moved to the nineteenth-century house fifteen years ago, there was no place inside to sit and connect with the natural surroundings. To solve the problem, Florence re-envisioned a rickety screened porch as a conservatory-style room. Keeping the footprint of the original porch, she added walls of windows, French doors with transoms, and crown moldings that bring the outdoors in while also complementing the proportions and style of the house. Although the architectural envelope is traditional, the interior marries the old with the new, combining contemporary and antique furnishings and accessories in a unified palette of white, lavender, and purple.

While the colors have a fresh, modern appeal, de Dampierre explains that the inspiration came from Tsarina Alexandra's bedroom in the Pavlosk palace in Russia. "Her bedroom was a very pretty shade of lavender, which is hard to achieve. If you don't get the right color, it looks horrible." Not surprisingly, the designer got the shade right, painting the walls a pale, vibrant lilac that is lovely whether surrounded by summer greenery or winter snow.

The luminous shade also highlights the room's antique furnishings, such as a nineteenth-century French nursing chair with pale hyacinth velvet upholstery that accentuates its dark mahogany arms and legs. The conservatory also includes a set of six American Empire klismos chairs designed by Benjamin Latrobe. Their matte black paint and faded gilding contrast with the shiny white glaze of a coffee table, designed by de Dampierre, in the shape of a giant tree stump. "Adding something unusual—an unexpected object or color—makes a room interesting," says the designer, who also added curtains appliquéd with ultra-suede Hollyhock leaves in various purple tones. While several other pieces in the room are also designed by de Dampierre, intriguing objects like a magenta Lalique butterfly and a tiered alabaster font are finds from local flea markets.

De Dampierre's other addition to the property is a neoclassical pool pavilion designed to complement Litchfield's Federal and Greek Revival architecture. Although its pediment and Ionic columns are traditional in style, the porch is deeper than usual, accommodating wicker sofas at either end and, in the center, a picnic table surrounded by antique French garden chairs. Here, friends gather for lunch or dinner amid a mix of colorful majolica plates and fine and not-so-fine crystal, glass, flatware, and serving pieces. When not in use, the majolica is stored in the pavilion's living room—an airy space with a pale-blue tray ceiling and open shelves where eighteenth-century French busts are juxtaposed with antique prints, intensely colored contemporary art, fantastical pottery, fine porcelain, and glass. "It all goes back to having a sense of humor in how you combine things and cultivating an adventurous use of color," says de Dampierre. "That is the essence of French chic."

OPPOSITE: *French doors with amber colored glass open from a formal sitting room to the luminous conservatory. The bold geometry of the carpet combines with designs inspired by nature—a coffee table resembling a tree trunk and curtains appliquéd with silk leaves.*

OPPOSITE: *The author of "Chairs: A History," de Dampierre is an avid collector of chairs, particularly those with strong character. Two of a set of six American Empire klismos chairs designed by Benjamin Latrobe are drawn up to the table.*

ABOVE: *The delicate lavender shade of the conservatory walls is echoed in amethyst-colored obelisks designed by de Dampierre and amethyst-colored goblets.*

ABOVE AND OPPOSITE: *White walls and furniture beneath a pale blue ceiling bring the outdoors inside the poolhouse, while the green-and-white stripes of the cushions and carpet create an outdoor room on the porch. White-painted French garden chairs and a rustic picnic table provide a foil for brightly colored vintage majolica and tinted stemware, including cranberry colored flutes and green water glasses. Pineapple lanterns designed by de Dampierre hold votive candles within as well as tapers on top. A vintage tea set inspired by summer's ripe tomatoes is a perfect accessory.*

A Personal Eye

Some houses make statements of style. Others tell stories, bearing witness to the experience, fascinations, and inheritance of their owners. Although their contents may be fine, these residences are not shaped by fashion or connoisseurship. Rather, they are tangible expressions of a personal eye—places filled with objects chosen not just for the sake of beauty, but also memory, meaning, and whim. In such residences, precious antiques share space with objects of no market value and curiosities from far afield mingle with familiar inherited things. All are treated with equal respect, combined in compositions that tell stories or provoke the imagination.

The houses embody the term eclectic, a word defined as the selection of ideas from varied of sources. Indicating an open-minded point of view, eclecticism points to a gift for perceiving beauty and meaning in likely and unlikely places. Whether choosing from goods in a distant souk or deciding which beloved heirloom to display, individuals with a strong personal eye bring this talent to the design of their homes. The following residences are filled with unusual juxtapositions of objects and materials. Beidermeier chairs sit on a wooly Moroccan rug, ormolu sconces illuminate rugged brick walls, pages from a 1920s encyclopedia paper a bedroom's walls, and Delft tile, American furniture, and roughly woven ethnic textiles combine in a truly international dining room. Each of these rooms reveals the personal eye of its creator, both through the objects within them and the unexpected ways in which they are combined.

Fearless Juxtaposition

Legendary architect of the Gilded Age, designer, tastemaker, and social dynamo, Stanford White was a larger-than-life man in a larger-than-life time. Drawing from an extensive vocabulary of classical, medieval, Romanesque, and vernacular styles, the houses he designed for America's leading families combined familiar elements in unexpected ways.

"He abandoned preconception and followed the guidance of his imagination," says his great-grandson Sam White, "perhaps at no place more completely than at Box Hill."

The architect's summer house on Long Island's North Shore, Box Hill was a retreat for his family, a weekend destination for fellow aesthetes and clients, and a creative laboratory. There, White expanded his vision and indulged his whims, transforming the original farmhouse into an eclectic collage where refined neoclassical details contrast with rugged pebbledash walls.

Sam, also an architect, describes his great-grandfather's approach to design as "fearless juxtaposition." This aesthetic finds powerful expression in the interior, where exposed steel beams, bamboo matting, Delft tiles, and eighteenth-century ecclesiastical pieces represent just a sampling of ingredients. Now owned by Sam's brother Daniel White, Box Hill remains remarkably as it was in his great-grandfather's day. "I've always loved the house," says Daniel, who grew up there from the age of eleven and moved back thirty years later.

Soon after Daniel took over, he married fashion executive Betsy Hussey, who became chief curator of the house, assisting not only in its restoration, but also in tracking down furnishings in attics, cupboards, and out-of-the-way places and returning them to their original places. "The house is well documented with photographs taken for Stanford White, so we know a lot about how he decorated, how the rooms were set up, and general atmosphere," she explains. The first room they restored was the dining room, where highly textured walls and leaded glass window frames were repainted and Delft tiles surrounding the fireplace, cleaned and repaired. Afterwards, Betsy layered ethnic textiles on the window seat and arranged pottery, china, and glass in windows, on walls, and shelves, recreating the setting in which the first generation of Whites entertained.

Next on the list was the voluminous "baroque room," where several massive gilded baroque columns once stood, appearing to support a ceiling covered with inexpensive reed matting. The columns are now in the front hall, but many original contents remain, including a French Renaissance mantel and a neoclassical baldacchino. When Betsy turned her attention to the china cabinet, originally belonging to Stanford White's mother, it was sorely in need of restoration. After it was repaired, she filled its shelves with blue-and-white china discovered beneath the dining room window seat. Months later, she found a small painting of the cabinet that depicted many of the same pieces she had placed.

"My approach has always been to respect the past while also bringing in new touches and ideas," explains Betsy, whose personal contributions are subtle but chic.

All the Whites agree that it's essential to conserve not only the contents of the house, but also its spirit. In Stanford and Bessie White's time, the rooms, porches, and gardens were always a work in progress, alive with family and friends. "When our parents lived here, it was also a place of celebration," Sam recalls. Thanks to the efforts of an entire family, Box Hill still has that sense of warmth and hospitality, surviving not as a memento of a lost moment in time, but as a tableau vivant infused with the vitality of its creator.

OPPOSITE: *An Italianate bust of indeterminate age rests on an American neoclassical sideboard, flanked by silver candelabra and elegant coupes de champagne.*

ABOVE AND LEFT: *With a ceiling medallion incorporating the mask of Apollo, a motif favored by Louis XVI, a wall of Delft tile, Japanese palace dogs, and an American gilded girandole mirror, the dining room displays an array of styles and materials. Walls are covered in Anaglypta, a cardboard pressed to resemble paneling or Spanish leather and painted white—an unusual aesthetic for the early 1900s.*

OPPOSITE: *Stanford and Bessie White's picnic blanket now covers the dining room window seat. The walls and windowsill display a collection of vintage majolica apothecary jars and plates interspersed with contemporary ceramics.*

ABOVE: *A bronze cast of Augustus Saint-Gaudens's wedding portrait of Bessie White hangs above a giltwood and marble console table, flanked by contemporary bronze lamps.*

ABOVE: *The arrangement of Willowware in a bureau bookcase, originally owned by Stanford White's mother, follows that in a painting by his daughter-in-law Laura Chanler White.*

ABOVE RIGHT: *A set of tea boxes decorated in black and gilt relate to the somber palette of the portrait above and the ebony inlay on the chest below.*

OPPOSITE: *Hand-colored plates from a volume of Renaissance portraits are grouped above an American demi-lune table. The silvered lamp, found at a Berlin antiques market, is a recent acquisition.*

OVERLEAF: *The Baroque Room exemplifies the "fearless juxtaposition" that characterized Stanford White's interiors. Inexpensive reed matting covers the walls and exposed steel beams decorated with Italian giltwood medallions span the ceiling. Furnishings include a chandelier combining antlers with a wooden figure of St. Barbara, a pair of gilded Italian torchieres flanking the massive carved fireplace, and a mix of American, English, and European furniture.*

Villa Albicini

"I love houses," declares native Charlestonian Tommy Bennett, a compulsive collector of furniture, decorative objects, and historic dwellings. Raised in a Federal house in the city's oldest neighborhood, he was fascinated by architecture from an early age, drawing houses on paper scraps and constructing them from Lego and wooden blocks. He joined the Preservation Society of Charleston by the age of twenty and soon after acquired a moldering eighteenth-century house with handsome paneling and a bit of a vermin problem. He went on to love, care for, and protect more than a dozen historic residences in Charleston, including the revered Pineapple Gate and Branford-Horry houses. The most famous building he has owned, however, lies far outside Charleston's city limits, in the vicinity of Versailles. Built by the French government in 1801, the neoclassical *petit palais* known as the Temple of Glory, became the twentieth-century home of Lord Oswald Guinness and his wife Lady Diana Mosley, the most beautiful and infamous of the Mitford sisters.

After selling the French villa, Bennett thought he'd never find another house to rival its beauty and romance—but then he discovered the Villa Albicini in Macon, Georgia.

"It's more fanciful than anything else I've seen in this country," he remarks.

When the house was designed in the 1920s by architects Philip Trammel Shutze and Neel Reid, it was sited on a bucolic piece of property cut from the Idle Hour horse farm and racetrack. With its expressive baroque facade with overblown pilasters, pinnacles, finials, and a split stair that makes the faded pink stucco building look more monumental than it is, the house projects a grand illusion. When Bennett first toured its rooms, however, the effect was less impressive. Although their shapes and proportions were dazzling, the rooms were filled with what he describes as French hotel furniture and a leatherette lazy-boy. "There was so much clutter, I had to ask the realtor to move

some furniture out of the house," he recalls. "Only then could I see its beautiful bones."

Although Bennett began collecting furniture for the house well before he moved in, his overall approach has been to keep things spare. "The rooms don't need a lot of furniture, but what you choose has to be strong," he explains. Among the pieces he selected are a 1725 French Regence commode and a Parsons-style coffee table with an early eighteenth-century Italian specimen marble top. These grace the sun parlor, a spacious room featuring Shutze's original marble parquet floor and Chinoiserie mural wallpaper installed in 1965 by interior designers David Byers and Charles Townsend of Brown and Company in Atlanta. They are also responsible for the modern mirrored wall, in which glass sconces and a baroque marble mantel reflect.

"I love neoclassical furniture, but the house is so over the top it just doesn't work there," observes Bennett, who chose pieces based on proportion and character rather than period or style. Arresting juxtapositions result, such as the Swedish dolphin console and Biedermeier sofa with ebonized swan arms in the entrance hall. Matching Biedermeier chairs stand on a shaggy Moroccan carpet in the living room, which also includes an Irish Regency mirror, George III faux-bamboo chairs, and modern metallic bamboo-form standing lamps. "I love anything bamboo because it's so exotic," says Bennett, who also found a mid-twentieth-century Jansen table with a zinc bamboo-style base for the sun parlor. He hasn't yet furnished the dining room, but is considering a modern granite-topped table with extremely simple lines. In the meantime, the room is empty, except for a single English Regency chair and a Venetian chandelier. "The architecture is so strong that it doesn't need much jewelry," says Bennett. "Even empty, the house sings."

OPPOSITE: *The sunroom stretches across the rear of the house, overlooking an Italianate garden. Mirrored panels extend the space and highlight decorative elements including the marble baroque-style mantel and blown-glass sconces.*

OPPOSITE: *The most extravagantly decorative piece of furniture in the house is an early nineteenth-century Swedish console with dazzling giltwood dolphins.*

ABOVE: *An Austrian or Russian Biedermeier sofa with ebonized swan-shaped arms stands in the entrance hall, with matching chairs in the adjoining living room. Above the door casing is a trompe l'oeil architectural fantasy.*

ABOVE: *Mounted on a modern Parsons-style base, a turn-of-the-eighteenth century specimen marble piece serves as the sunroom's coffee table. Across the room, a map made by Piranesi for Robert Adam hangs above a French Regence chest.*

OPPOSITE: *While Bennett attempts to reclaim the original mantelpiece, the dining room remains empty except for a Venetian glass chandelier and English Regency chair.*

ABOVE: *A 1950s French coffee table, Biedermeier swan chairs, George III faux-bamboo chairs, and a Moroccan rug happily co-exist in the living room. With its original glass intact, an Irish Regency mirror shaped like a snake swallowing its tail is the finest antique in the room.*

OPPOSITE: *A Louis XVI desk, previously installed in the Temple of Glory's drawing room, perfectly fits a bay in the Villa Albicini living room. A marbleized-paper-bound biography of General Victor Moreau, for whom the Temple of Glory was built, is another souvenir of Bennett's earlier residence. Silver and hardstone snuffboxes and a marble specimen are arranged on the oxblood leather surface.*

Curatorial Style

A utilitarian brick structure built in the mid-nineteenth century to house the waterworks in Macon, Georgia, Chris Howard and Carey Pickard's residence poses a distinct contrast to the pretty Victorian cottages surrounding it. This juxtaposition is the first of many that combine to create a crazy quilt of collective and personal history throughout the house and grounds. "We don't subscribe to the 'everything has to work together' school of design," says Pickard.

"I don't think everything in here *does* work together, but if you look carefully, you can pick up on relationships between things and the stories they tell."

A composition of bibelots arranged on top of a table inherited from a friend illustrates the point. Including a bronze obelisk Howard purchased from Louisiana antiquarian and friend Peter Patout, a vase Pickard bought from Southern outsider artist Howard Finster, and an array of boxes picked up on trips abroad, the arrangement is a three-dimensional travel log.

Considering that both men are preservationists and historians, it's not surprising that their approach to decorating is curatorial. "Like many Southerners, I was born into a family of storytellers," Pickard explains. "The objects I grew up with were tangible links to the past and to ancestors I'd never even met." Although Howard is not Southern by birth, he converted in his teens to its culture of memory after discovering a copy of *Ghosts of the Mississippi* at a second-hand bookstore. He studied preservation at Tulane University and has subsequently worked with nearly every historical and preservation organization in Macon.

That involvement has also made it easier for Howard to acquire a bit of history for himself, including a crystal chandelier offered at a benefit auction by Historic Macon Foundation. From the elegant home of a local grande dame,

the chandelier now hangs from the rugged wood ceiling of their brick-walled dining room. It's one of only a few purchased pieces in a room that is largely furnished by hand-me-down chairs, tables, and silver, including sterling and plated presentation pieces. "A lot of silver snobs look down their noses at presentation pieces," says Howard, "but I cherish them because they remind me of the people I come from and the things that they've done." Among the brightly polished pieces are a 1956 Bible school prize and a tray inscribed from J. Edgar Hoover to his grandfather, a former FBI agent.

The silver in the room is not just for display. It is not uncommon for the dinner table to be set for twelve with Irish linen napkins, silver goblets and bread plates, and sterling flatware in the Chantilly pattern. "It's not my favorite," says Pickard, "but it belonged to my grandmother, so I love it." During cocktail parties, a sizeable collection of silver julep cups, many engraved to commemorate special occasions, gets a workout as well. "It's more festive to drink out of them than ordinary glasses," remarks Howard, who keeps a stash in the bar tucked into a corner of the living room. Like the dining room, this room has brick walls, but that hasn't stopped the couple from hanging an eighteenth-century chandelier from the ceiling and mounting ormolu sconces above the rustic mantel.

"We don't take our things too seriously," says Howard. "It's fun to hang a gilded sconce on a crumbling brick wall." Pickard agrees. "I admire houses where every detail is as it would have been in a certain year, but that's not the life we've chosen. We've layered in things from many people, places, and times." Howard adds, "It all comes back to storytelling. That's how we keep history alive."

OPPOSITE: *The eclectic display on the living room mantel includes a landscape and a still life by unknown painters and a portrait of Pickard's grandmother. Gilded sconces from a New York City penthouse flank a Suzani discovered at the International Folk Art Market in Santa Fe.*

PRECEDING SPREAD: *Spanning the entire front of the waterworks, the living room is divided into three seating areas. A Venetian chest, flanked by Regency-style side chairs, backs up to the sofa facing the fireplace, while an eighteenth-century English chandelier hangs over a center table piled with books. Paintings and portraits by regional artists enliven the walls and bookcases.*

ABOVE: *A nineteenth-century mahogany tilt-top table holds a profusion of exotic objects — boxes of silver, boule, and semi-precious jewels, branches of coral, a spiraled ammonite, Indonesian shadow puppets, a Chinese figure, and an obelisk. "The objects are grouped by color," says Pickard, "but what is more important to us is the relationships between these things and memories they hold."*

ABOVE LEFT: *A Lucite box filled with dirt from Graceland, Kenyan boar tusks, and contemporary porcelain pieces including a vase by Jonathan Adler offer a study in white and beige atop a contemporary glass-top table.*

ABOVE: *Frequently used glassware, silver goblets, and julep cups line the shelves of the bar area.*

ABOVE LEFT: *A panoply of silverware arranged in a biscuit box includes a sugar shell, several grapefruit spoons, and a pierced olive spoon.*

ABOVE: *A Victorian marble-topped table and alabaster lamp from Pickard's childhood home now grace the dining room. Much of the silver displayed on the table comes from his family, including compotes, cigarette holders, and a bowl given to his mother when she made her debut.*

OPPOSITE: *In the dining room, a crystal chandelier and a sizeable collection of silver serving pieces glitter against a humble backdrop of painted brick and grass cloth. Artichokes arranged in julep cups add a bit of whimsy to the formal table setting.*

ABOVE: *Commissioned from the late Ola Mae Ford, an African-American quilter from Macon, the quilt on the bed is made from scraps of vintage men's suits in a masculine mix of blues, grays, and browns.*

OPPOSITE: *Antique men's grooming tools, including brushes and a silver shoe horn, share the top of a mahogany dresser with old leather boxes filled with collar stays and cufflinks. A nineteenth-century gilded mirror with overscaled fleur-de-lis ornament hangs above.*

Unknown Provenance

David Braly and Mark Montoya are a little sketchy about the provenance of some of the objects in their house, possibly because both are pencil-wielding artists rather than antiques experts. Braly, an architect with McAlpine Tankersley Architecture, is also a muralist whose classically inspired scenes have graced interiors by leading design professionals. Montoya, a garden designer and former product designer, finds inspiration in both antique architecture and nature. Together, the two renovated an early-twentieth-century fire station in Montgomery, creating a light-filled studio on the ground floor and a suite of rooms above.

Both work in the studio, where renderings in progress are mounted on a partition wall, but the office behind the wall is largely Braly's domain. There he can quote the provenance of almost every item, including a drafting table identical to the one Frank Lloyd Wright used, made by The Post Company and purchased in Hudson, New York. He can also attest that the multi-volume set of *The Domestic Architecture of England,* featuring detailed plates of English architecture, was once in the library of John Russell Pope. But ask him about the print hanging on a door, and all he can tell you is that it's Russian and that he bought it in a Moscow flea market.

"As a rule, we don't collect things based on origin—when they were made, or where, or by whom," Montoya explains. "We acquire them because of their beauty, their shape, and the memories they hold."

On the walls of the upstairs hall, prints of ancient monuments combine with classical busts and architectural fragments. Although some are valuable, no antiquarian would deem everything in the space "important." The pair of large Moroccan jars is contemporary—a souvenir from a trip to North Africa. Despite its crusty patina, the William Kent-ish garden urn at one end of the hall it is a faux-antique selected for the beauty of its classical form. Braly and Montoya know little about the Oriental carpet, but they can say a lot about the prints, including an engraving of a section of St. Paul's in London and a Piranesi etching of Hadrian's Villa outside Rome "I became very interested in engravings while I was studying architectural history at Cambridge," says Braly. His work reflects the influence of these images of Greek and Roman monuments, as demonstrated by a mural in the stairwell depicting a fluted Corinthian column from the temple of Castor and Pollux in Rome. Much larger in scale than the actual column, the mural transforms the stairwell's irregular plaster walls into a dramatic decorative feature.

Montoya achieved an equally remarkable metamorphosis in the master bedroom by papering its walls with pages from a 1920s edition of the Grolier encyclopedia. With pages oriented sideways and white margins forming mortar-like lines, the composition creates the impression of masonry blocks. Although the original plan called for pages with text only, Montoya began discovering images of familiar birds, plants, sculpture, and buildings and changed his scheme. "The walls became a scrapbook," he says. The three-dimensional still life he and Braly arranged on top of the dining table is equally autobiographical, with feathers and lichen collected on walks, a plate from Florence, a wooden salt bowl carved by a mutual friend, and a silver tray and candlesticks from Braly's family home.

OPPOSITE: *A large studio now occupies the space where the fire engines once parked. Montoya transformed a structural column into a sculpture by wrapping it with driftwood collected at nearby Lake Martin.*

OPPOSITE AND ABOVE: *A long hall runs like a spine through the second-floor living quarters. Inspired by seventeenth-century houses in Amsterdam, Braly selected two shades of brown for the walls and a darker shade for the ceiling. Accessed by a narrow stair hall, the space is densely fitted with antique prints, antique French corbels transformed into sconces, and new Moroccan jars flanking a German sofa. Braly embellished the stair hall with a mural based on the Corinthian capitals of Temple of Castor and Pollux in Rome.*

OVERLEAF: *A copy of a 1730s London map covers one wall of the office. The bookcase serves as a divider, with volumes on neoclassical architecture and antiquities accessible from both sides.*

ABOVE: *In the dining room, eighteenth-century French designs for organ pipe enclosures hang above a Chinese screen. English Queen Anne chairs with cabriole legs and a vase-form splats and Delft pottery on the mantel complete the eclectic decor.*

OPPOSITE: *The living room is filled with unusual objects, including a piece of antique equipment designed for shaping carriage wheels and a Corinthian capital salvaged from a demolition site. Inspired by an antique Dutch precedent, Braly designed a chandelier updated with Edison bulbs and a gazing ball. Piranesi etchings hang behind the fire pole and a menorah-shaped wood object, perhaps once a lamp, stands in the opposite corner.*

Country Life

Antiques have long been a part of country life in America—although in centuries past, they weren't antiques—they were simply what was available at the time, whether primitive country-made pieces or refined furnishings manufactured for well-to-do farmers and merchants. Period rooms in the great country houses of England and America tend to give the impression that country life can be stiff and formal. Fortunately, we also have the pages of *English Country Life* and *World of Interiors* to remind us that laid-back ease and eccentricities can also characterize the decoration of country houses. At its most delightful, country house style combines the formal with the relaxed in unstudied assemblages of mismatched antiques and cherished family heirlooms. Furnishings and art are chosen not so much to impress, as to please the eye of the inhabitants and to endow rooms with comfort and charm.

The houses featured are disparate in style, but they share certain hallmarks. One is Federal Connecticut dwelling where three generations of a family have shaped spaces reflecting their personal styles. One room is filled with Queen Anne and William and Mary antiques, another with an international mélange of antiques, and a third with primitive American pieces. In a nearby farmhouse, a well-known interior designer combines sophisticated colors with rural English antiques to create a chic take on country style. Inherited pieces and primitive Southern antiques furnish the rooms of an Alabama plantation house decorated by an artist, preservationist, and antiques dealer who understands how to create quirky, personal expressions using elements from the past. By harvesting finds from flea markets, antiques shops, and their own attics, and bringing a spirit of whimsy to the process, these homeowners prove that it's possible to decorate country houses with panache.

Country in the City

Although it is only fifteen minutes from downtown Birmingham, Alabama, Mary and Ed Finch's house has all the charm of a bijou villa in the French Riviera. Built in 1926, when English Tudor was the prevailing style in Birmingham's garden suburbs, the Finches' house is a bit harder to pin down stylistically. "I love how it feels like a country house, particularly the way faces away from the street and toward the woods," says Mary Finch. "As soon as I saw it, I knew I was meant to live here." Moving from a Georgian-style house, also built in 1926 but in a far more formal style, she was not entirely sure how well her transplanted furnishings would work in the more relaxed setting. But soon one of her axioms as an interior decorator proved true.

"If you have good things that you love and know how to put them together, they'll look great in any setting."

Relegating her dressiest furnishings in the more formal living room, Mary Finch combined more relaxed pieces, including several country French antiques, in an adjoining room where the family spends most of its time. This long rectangular space was designed as a sleeping porch, but serves perfectly as a family sitting room with a dining room at one end. Walls of windows with woodland views wrap the room and French doors open to a terrace overlooking a boxwood parterre. Although there is enough space in the house for a separate dining room, the Finches decided to nestle their table next the bank of windows commanding the best view of Birmingham's rolling hills.

The large Agra carpet once belonged to a dear friend. "That old worn rug has a lot of sentimental value," says Finch, who used its red and ivory palette to inspire her fabric choices, including the checked fabric on a pair of provincial French bergeres. Linen curtains with a Chinoiserie pattern in shades of rose and beige further demonstrate the decorator's talent for mixing colors and patterns. Softening

the rooms walls and windows, the curtains provide a backdrop for a large carved stag's head discovered in a flea market. To connect the room with its woodland surroundings, Finch chose a shade of lichen green for the ceiling and placed a small Italian chandelier with colorful porcelain flowers in the center. Although she admits the delicate chandelier was an unlikely choice for the room, Finch says, "I loved it and I knew I could make it work."

Reminiscent of fine French country houses, the master bedroom is furnished with early nineteenth-century French armchairs and a Chinoiserie étagère filled with eighteenth-century creamware. In the nearby hall, a late-eighteenth-century Welsh cupboard displaying rare brown and yellow English Ridgway pottery recalls the contents of nineteenth-century English country houses. "I find it almost impossible to pass up a good china, glassware, and linens," admits Mary, who stores her overflow in a walk-in china cabinet and an Anglo-Indian linen press.

Whether setting tables in the family room, on the balcony, or in the garden, Finch likes to mix the formal with the relaxed, to create a sophisticated country mood. One favorite setting for the indoor dining table combines brown-and-white transferware, majolica ornaments, Mexican glass, Tiffany silver, and antique etched stemware. Finch also likes mixing formal with rustic accoutrements when dining in the garden. For al fresco parties, she often combines fine antique silver with contemporary pottery on a toile quilt unfurled across a long stone table. When the table decoration is complete with a flower arrangement composed within a hollow log, Finch's vision is fulfilled in a magical way. "This is the way I show people I love them," says the homeowner, who is happiest when sharing the delights of her country home in the city with family and with friends.

OPPOSITE: *The dining table is set in woodland tones, with mid-nineteenth-century English transferware, Mexican etched green glass stemware, and green linens that complement a soft arrangement of hydrangeas in a majolica cachepot.*

OPPOSITE AND ABOVE: *A red and ivory Agra carpet inspired the palette for the living room's patterned linen curtains, striped seat covers, and plaid upholstered chairs. A late-nineteenth-century Black Forest carving of a stag's head with antique reindeer bells enhances the European country atmosphere of the room. Chunky pottery lamps made from whiskey and gin barrels contrast with the delicate design of an Italian chandelier with porcelain flowers and painted leaves.*

ABOVE: *Customized elements in the kitchen include an open cupboard made of reclaimed oak above the stove and limestone countertops stained with coffee and finished with beeswax. Displays of English Ridgway plates and transferware and antique cooking implements contribute to the cozy atmosphere. The Dutch door offers views to the garden.*

ABOVE: *Finch transformed a breakfast nook into a china closet and butler's pantry that holds a colorful array of china, including aqua glazed English Calyx Ware, early Spode, Royal Crown Derby Old Avesbury, and Chelsea Bird by Copeland, and a collection of tinted stemware.*

OPPOSITE AND ABOVE: *Covered with Hodsoll McKenzie floral cotton with an intentionally faded, tea-stained appearance, the irregular walls of the master bedroom appear as though they have been untouched for decades. An eighteenth-century French mirror and pair of bergeres covered in hand-loomed French silk complete the fantasy. An English black-lacquer étagère shows off the delicate borders of basket-weave creamware.*

ABOVE LEFT: *The turquoise-painted interior of an English oak Welsh cupboard accentuates the scalloped edges of a collection of rare brown and yellow English Ridgway. Horn cups and a copper samovar add more rich tones to the handsome tableau.*

ABOVE RIGHT: *A lifetime's collection of napkins, placemats, and table-cloths are stored in an Anglo-Indian linen press. Tags indicate how many and what type are in each stack and ribbons keep the linens from wrinkling.*

ABOVE: *In the garden, an antique French iron console presides over a table set with Tiffany flatware, Mexican stemware, and contemporary pottery.*

Country Finery

When a pair of house-lovers and antiques collectors purchased a modest 1960s cottage in Highlands, North Carolina, as their second home, its most compelling feature was the beautiful setting of old-growth rhododendron, mountain laurel, and oaks. With an awkward entrance sequence, small rooms chopped up into even smaller ones, sheetrock walls, and low ceilings, the interior posed a number challenges, but the new owners were happy to take them on. Before long, they transformed the simple cottage into a stylish retreat combining relaxed Southern charm with a touch of English country house decorum. To start, they created an inviting living room by removing a partition wall and raising the ceiling up to the rooftop. Next, they applied shiplap pine boards to walls and tongue-and-groove paneling to ceilings throughout the house. Painted a creamy shade of white, the new old-fashioned cladding provided the ideal backdrop for a collection of antique furnishings the couple had been assembling for years. The final touch—a primitive Georgia mantel with vestiges of mossy green paint—created a much needed focal point in the living room and injected a touch of color echoing the woodland setting.

Decorated with nineteenth-century French papier-maché face screens, English transferware platters, creamware pitchers, and Staffordshire lambs, the country-style mantel is unexpectedly elegant in its garniture. "We love the surprise of putting something formal in a country house," explains the collector, who also mounted a baroque-style mirror above a rustic Southern table, beneath which he stacked split firewood. Gilt framed prints of historic English personages and an eighteenth-century French bergere add formal notes to the living room. These are balanced by more laid-back textiles including unfigured linen on the camelback sofa and a kilim layered on top of a sisal rug.

Originally, the front door of the cottage opened directly into this room, offering little in the way of ceremony. The owners recently solved this problem by reconfiguring the facade to feature a new entrance with a handsome antique door opening to a tiny foyer.

This small addition provided opportunities to integrate more antiques, both inside and outside the house. Salvaged material including an Indian door, French louvered shutters, and a pair of columns topped by urns, adds distinction to the new entrance.

"We are often drawn to things because of their patina," observes the collector. "Patina instantly adds a feeling of romance and age."

The couple looked no further than their own primary residence, an antebellum cottage in Macon, Georgia, to source the richly colored pine boards lining the interior of the new foyer. Salvaged when they dismantled the root cellar, the boards still bear vestiges of white paint that complement the chalky finish of the chandelier illuminating the space.

Although they share a penchant for unexpected touches of finery, like the foyer's chandelier, the couple rarely strays too far from country style. Antique baskets and a pair of cane rug-beaters hang on the foyer walls, carved-wood deer heads with natural antlers can be found throughout the house, and a palette of brown and green with accents of orange reflects the seasonal woodland setting. In keeping with low-key Southern style, wicker is the predominant material on the large all-season porch. The wicker seating is new, but its traditional design and faded toile upholstery impart the appearance of age. Older wicker pieces, including a pair of painted tables and an antique twig table add a touch of quirk, as do the primitive antique sideboard and carved Victorian chairs in the dining area. "We want to enjoy being where we are and celebrate its natural beauty, but not at the expense of elegance and charm," says the collector. "Decorating gets pretty boring when it's uniformly rustic," her husband agrees. "We like to mix in finer things."

OPPOSITE: *Flanked by weathered French shutters and Doric columns capped with urns, an antique Indian door hints at the sophisticated take on country living expressed within.*

LEFT: *Furnished with antique furniture and new and vintage wicker, the porch combines relaxed country style with a touch of formality. A carpet made from strips of kilims adds a dash of color to the overall brown-and-white palette.*

ABOVE: *The elements of the entrance porch offer a study in patina.*

OPPOSITE: *Wood reclaimed from the root cellar of the owners' Georgia house covers the walls of the foyer, where the worn surface is juxtaposed with an ornate chandelier, tole trays, and a gilded laurel wreath. A set of stacking metal shelves displays a collection of baskets, books, and miscellany accumulated over the years.*

ABOVE: *Removing a dropped ceiling and partition wall and adding new painted-pine paneling transformed a pair of cramped rooms into a cozy sitting area. The residents established a natural woodland palette by mixing bamboo with a variety of wood tones and incorporating shades of green and orange. The juxtaposition of a gilded mirror with a primitive Georgia table perfectly expresses the owners' rustic-meets-refined aesthetic.*

Fancy and Plain

When artist, designer, preservationist, and antiques dealer Barbara Adkins saw the opportunity to keep her ancestors' home in the family, she seized it, even though the prospects of restoring it were daunting. Occupied by an elderly great aunt, the house in Harpersville, Alabama, was nearly derelict and in danger of being vandalized, thanks to rumors of cash stashed beneath the floorboards. To protect the family home, Adkins moved in the day after her aunt died. Returning to the place where she recalled sharing farm-style meals in the kitchen and rambling in the surrounding fields, she discovered a freezing cold relic with naked light bulbs hanging from leaky ceilings and drafty rooms with shredded wallpaper.

"I was the only one in my family interested in restoring the house," Adkins says. "I could see its potential when everyone else thought it was hopeless." Today, the 1840s vernacular Greek Revival house is structurally sound, centrally heated, and lovingly restored in the spirit of a home lived in and loved by generations. A few important original family pieces remain in the house, including an early-nineteenth-century South Carolina table and two Alabama folk art portraits, as well as less fine but equally cherished heirlooms. These are combined with objects assembled by Adkins, a lifetime collector and owner of Harpersville's Black Sheep Antiques shop, who combines a keen eye for form, quality, and period style with a quirky personal sensibility.

"Anybody can have a museum—I'm more interested in unexpected juxtapositions," she says. "I like to blend the fancy with the not-so-fancy, and I'm not afraid to mix in something contemporary."

In the dining room, the polished surface of an elegant banquet table contrasts with the worn gray paint of the heart-pine floor. A rustic corner cabinet lacking a drawer but retaining original glass panes displays blue-and-white china in patterns common to Southern plantations. When Adkins sets the table, she intersperses these with modern plates and glasses and a mismatched selection of coin-silver flatware. On a side table, a pair of Parisian painted lamps offers striking contrast to prints hanging above depicting sinister looking black birds. Combined with a glimpse of the vintage undertaker's sign that decorates the adjoining dogtrot hallway, these hint at the Southern gothic. Such intersections of old and new, primitive and refined are found throughout the house, where Adkins has preserved the past while also reserving the right to be herself.

The most modern moment in the house occurs in the kitchen, where a graphic grid of shelves designed by Adkins and built by her father covers one large wall. White paint accentuates the shapes, colors, and textures of the objects filling them, including antique crockery, decoys, books, and baskets. The shelves also draw attention to a doorway in the middle of the wall framing a view into the master bedroom, where one of the folk portraits gazes out from above the mantel. The kitchen also features a new island with a four-inch thick slab of Alabama white marble that adds another modern element to the room where Adkins remembers drinking hand-churned buttermilk produced by the plantation cows.

Now, as then, this is the most used room in the house—a place where the family, joined by two rescue dogs and a cat called Fat Girl, dines, dozes, reads, works, and steps out to the adjacent porch to catch the evening breeze. "It's a great place to live," says Sonny Adkins, who admits he suspected his future wife was out of her mind when she first showed him the house. "But I knew her well enough to realize that she could do it, would do it, and do it correctly."

OPPOSITE: *The passage between the kitchen wing and dining room features a Georgia-made huntboard in "country Sheraton" style and a tradesman's sign with lettering hand-painted on a window screen.*

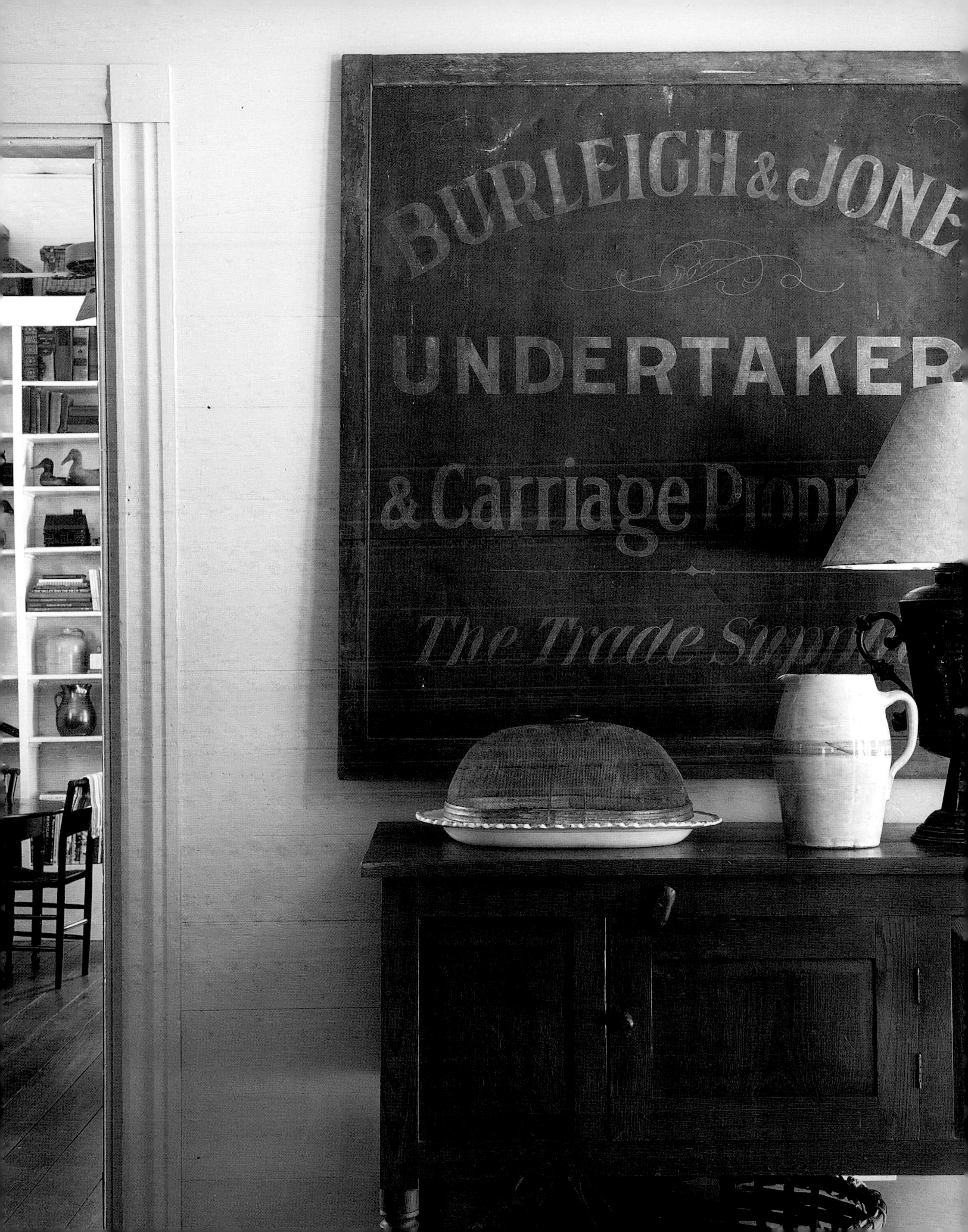
BURLEIGH & JONE
UNDERTAKER
& Carriage Propri
The Trade Supp

PRECEDING SPREAD: *A collection of duck decoys, pottery, and American folk art is displayed on the kitchen shelves.*

ABOVE AND OPPOSITE: *Heirlooms in the dining room include a c. 1820 drop-leaf table with legs carved in a rice motif, brought to Alabama from South Carolina by Adkins's ancestors, and an 1834 portrait of her great-great-great grandfather's third wife as an infant. Rush-bottom chairs surround an elegant Sheraton-style banquet table, demonstrating the prevailing "fancy and plain" approach to design. English Willowware and featheredge plates and platters typical of early-nineteenth-century Southern plantation tableware adorn the shelves of an unassuming corner cabinet.*

ABOVE: *In the master bedroom, an 1834 portrait of one of the farm-house's original residents hangs above a vernacular Federal-style mantel. The rope bed in the rustic room also dates from the 1830s.*

OPPOSITE: *A monogrammed antique linen sheet with scalloped edges is mixed with contemporary linens to create a luxuriously inviting bed in the guest room. The Jenny Lind spool bed is original to the house.*

ABOVE: *With walls made of recycled windows and floors of slate, the summerhouse next to the garden serves as an airy living space, greenhouse, and art studio. In one corner of the long room, an antique drafting table and stool provides an inspiring place to sketch. A cozy sitting area includes a vintage wicker sofa with handmade pillows found in local tag sales.*

ABOVE: *In the center of the room, a cast iron garden table with original paint holds a collection of garden books. Tin watering cans, wire and wicker baskets, and bell jars all find use in the nearby garden.*

The Element of Surprise

When interior designer and author Annie Kelly and her husband, photographer Tim Street-Porter, decided to buy a second home, they started their search in Paris. "We were looking for an eighteenth-century apartment that would offer a contrast to our house in Los Angeles," says Kelly. But when a friend pointed out that there were plenty of eighteenth-century houses on the East Coast, they reset their sights on Connecticut. Before long, the couple acquired a farmhouse in Litchfield County with all the quirks of age: wide floorboards that creak a bit, old plaster walls that are slightly out of plumb, and original mantels that lean a little to one side. "It was the right size and the right period," says Kelly, who liked the fact that the building predated the American Revolution and would have housed English or European settlers.

One of the designer's credos is to furnish a house appropriately to its period and style. Then, she says, the interior will harmonize with its setting.

"We've always been drawn to early English and European furniture and objects, and this house provided the correct setting."

"That's not to say you can't add pieces from different periods to contribute character and make things more interesting," Her Connecticut cottage is a perfect illustration of this philosophy. Although the first impression is one of stepping back in time, something slightly unexpected appears in almost every room. A Doric column topped with a bronze finial stands just inside the front door—a salvaged bit of classical architecture contrasting with the interior's rustic simplicity. In a living room with hand-hewn ceiling beams and a primitive pine mantel, a black-and-white striped carpet provides an island of contemporary style. Slightly brighter than the pea-green shade popular in colonial America, chartreuse curtains add another up-to-date touch. While the English and European furniture is in sync with the house's period, a giant, sun-bleached elk horn poised on a low stool interjects a modern, almost sculptural element.

The couple's penchant for unlikely pairings of the high and the low, the natural and the hand-crafted finds full expression in the two bookcases framing the entrance to the dining room. On their shelves, books rub shoulders with antique children's toys, coral branches and shells, porcelain bowls, wooden boxes, and architectural fragments. Nearly all come from local antiques shows and flea markets. As a photographer, Street-Porter often finds inspiration in these places where, he says, "I'm always discovering compositions of things that are completely arresting because they are so unexpected and so unplanned." The local antiques scene is equally inspiring to Kelly: "If you want to find something fresh, lively, and individual, flea markets are the best places to look."

For the dining room, Kelly bought chairs in different but related styles, one associated with Yorkshire County and the other with Lancashire. Framed prints depicting English cultural and political figures appear to be hung on ribbons matching the red trim, but in reality Kelly painted the faux-ribbons to add a touch of whimsy.

At first, Kelly resisted the blue-and-white china so readily and cheaply available in the local shops and flea markets. But finally she succumbed, amassing a mix-and-match collection of English and Chinese transferware to complement the pieces her husband inherited from his English family. She likes to introduce an element of surprise by using empty decanters like obelisks to add height and glitter to table settings or mixing tinted modern glassware with finer crystal. "You should never be afraid to use something that's not 'correct,' especially if it captures your eye and your imagination," Kelly explains. "Otherwise things become too serious."

OPPOSITE: *In the living room, an antique demijohn balanced on the seat of a seventeenth- or eighteenth-century European chair catches the light. The chair is intentionally paired with an antique trunk with similar decorative carving.*

ABOVE: *A "married piece" combining a seventeenth-century chest with an eighteenth-century base conceals a drinks cabinet in a corner of the living room. The high-backed chair and column function as a subtle divider between the living room and entrance hall.*

PRECEDING SPREAD: *A tufted ottoman and new wing chairs with traditional silhouettes soften the rustic wood and plaster surfaces of the living room. Toile pillows combine with the striped carpet, inlaid box, and wool throw to add graphic energy. White bowls, shells, eggs, and coral branches mingle with books on the room's well-curated shelves.*

OPPOSITE: *Kelly and Street-Porter constantly tinker with the compositions of books, decorative objects, and curiosities that fill the living room bookshelves. "Getting the balance and proportions right is a delightful challenge," says Kelly. "It's about creating a tension between the books and the objects. Sometimes the books win and sometimes the objects do."*

OPPOSITE AND ABOVE: *Old plaster walls trimmed with red paint endow the dining room with character and warmth. Eighteenth-century prints, which appear to hang from faux-painted ribbons, and a nineteenth-century English portrait enliven the room. Kelly integrated blue-and-white transferware plates into the scheme to vary the geometric rhythm of prints and introduce more color and pattern.*

ABOVE: *With its simple but well-crafted furnishings, including a gate-leg table and a Swedish china cabinet, the morning room is a perfect expression of gentleman farmer style. Accentuating the irregular ceiling line, a stenciled border adds rural charm that contrasts with the opulence of full-length taffeta curtains.*

OPPOSITE: *A small alcove off the morning room provides storage for tableware, including crystal decanters frequently employed as obelisks in table settings and dark-brown jugs and blue-and-white china that carry out the predominant colors in the house.*

The Collected House

Collectors are rarely obsessed simply with objects—they are fascinated by the milieu in which they were created, the craftsmen who made them, and the people who owned them. They are collectors not just of things, but also of time and history. While beauty may be paramount, the narratives conveyed by the objects they acquire are equally important. Even when we know the history of a piece—its maker, its provenance—there are still mysteries that remain concealed. What events did it witness? To what conversations was it privy? Every time we hold an object from an earlier time, we connect with all the others who touched it before. That is why the homes of collectors are so engaging. We are captivated not only by the highly crafted details and the patina of the pieces surrounding us, but also by their stories. Little is more evocative than a portrait from which the subject gazes with eloquent eyes, but a small piece of hand-worked linen can be just as intriguing. For whom was it made, and by whom, and on what occasion?

The collectors featured here fall into several categories. One is multi-generational family of antiques dealers who have followed their passions from New England to Italy, furnishing a Connecticut farmhouse with the spoils of their adventures. Others are collectors of place and time—antiquarians obsessed with the material history of a specific region and a particular era. Another pair of collectors found a new home in a contemporary high-rise condominium for portraits, furniture, and decorative objects acquired over a lifetime. All of these connoisseurs demonstrate the timeless charisma of antiques and the varied ways we can integrate them into our lives.

Heirlooms of Place

There are only a few family heirlooms in the East Hampton weekend house of fashion executives Charles Keller and Glenn Purcell. Instead, the 1898 cedar-shake cottage is furnished with heirlooms of place—objects fabricated in the area or once owned by local families—which together form an unofficial museum of material history. "As soon as we bought the house, we began searching for furniture and objects that were local," Keller explains. This quest required expeditions to auctions, antiques shops, and yard sales, where the early bird most definitely gets the worm or, in this case, the rarest pieces of furniture and art, decorative objects, historic artifacts, and ephemera with local provenance.

Soon after buying the house, Keller and Purcell made a discovery that gave them a particular focus and ultimately led to a major collecting obsession. "We became intrigued when we heard that the Dominy family once lived around the corner from our house," says Purcell, referring to a revered family of East Hampton furniture makers that flourished between 1760 and 1840, fashioning chairs, tables, candle stands, beds, and even clocks for area residents. Now Keller and Purcell own representative pieces of nearly every type and period—some picked up at roadside sales and others at major New York auctions.

"It's our goal to identify and document the furniture," explains Purcell. "We are trying to keep these important pieces of local history from being lost."

The collection also includes paintings and prints by artists attracted to the beauty of the place in the nineteenth century, including Thomas Moran and his wife, Mary Nimmo Moran, Greenport resident Whitney Myron Hubbard, and Sag Harbor portraitist Orlando Hand Bears. Books from local family libraries and silver fabricated by eighteenth-century Southampton silversmith Elias Pelletreau and early-nineteenth-century East Hampton silversmith David Hedges are also featured. In most cases, Keller and Purcell know who made the objects, and often they can identify the families for whom they were made.

Even though the house is filled with museum-quality pieces, its rooms are not stuffy period-style displays. The cottage postdates most of its contents, which largely fall into the Federal and Empire periods. The dining room is filled almost exclusively with Dominy Empire furniture, including a rare set of six matched chairs, but in the adjoining living room, Austrian Biedermeier pieces share space with a mid-nineteenth-century sideboard Purcell inherited from his family in Newnan, Georgia. In the upstairs hall, a tightly composed hanging of small works of art and artifacts includes a vintage postcard of a view of Sag Harbor painted by local artist Annie Cooper Boyd, a model of a tall clock, silhouettes found in yard sales, and framed notes from friends who have visited.

"Many homes in the area are furnished with pieces drawn from a variety of periods, which is natural when family heirlooms are mixed in with more recent acquisitions," Keller observes. "The furnishing of our house feels layered and authentic." The Dominy dining table is often set with antique china and glassware, combined with contemporary Christofle flatware purchased in Paris. Whimsical arrangements of shells, Victorian curiosity domes, and sailor's valentines decorate guest bedrooms. Mid-twentieth-century leather club chairs offer comfortable seating in a room also graced by an 1830 portrait of a Sag Harbor ship captain. A personal homage to a beloved place, Keller and Purcell's house is not only a tribute to its past but also a celebration of its present as a place to relax and enjoy time with friends.

OPPOSITE: *Reference books, including "With Hammer in Hand," the definitive volume on the Dominy family, and "East Hampton History and Genealogy," share a tiger-maple Pembroke table attributed to Nathaniel Dominy V with a whaling log from the 1830s or 1840s.*

PRECEDING SPREAD: *Dominy furniture in the dining room includes an 1819 cherry dining table surrounded by a rare set of Dominy Empire chairs, c. 1810. Two more Dominy chairs in the Queen Anne splat-back style, date from the late eighteenth century. Artwork in the room includes a collection of etchings and paintings by artists who worked in the area, including a large seascape by James Gale Tyler and works by Whitney Myron Hubbard, Edward and Mary Nimmo Moran, and Arthur Turnbull Hill.*

ABOVE: *An eclectic collection of tableware includes contemporary Christofle flatware in the Malmaison pattern, nineteenth-century Limoges oyster shooters repurposed as salt cellars, and a hand-blown wine funnel.*

OPPOSITE: *Cranberry glass bowls, pink-and-white English transfer-ware plates, one embellished with a scene of a shipwreck, and vintage linens are local finds. Blue Venetian glass inherited by Keller and silver spoons by East Hampton silversmith David Hedges, arranged in a crystal salt dish, surround a well-provisioned cheeseboard.*

PRECEDING SPREAD: *Combining Long Island antiques with Austrian Biedermeier chairs, midcentury leather club chairs, and a contemporary roll-arm sofa, the living room is easily the most eclectic room in the house. A portrait by Abraham Dominy Tuthill of Sag Harbor whaling captain Isaac Hand hangs above a mid-nineteenth-century sideboard from Purcell's Georgia family.*

OPPOSITE: *On the dresser is a pair of eighteenth-century silver and sapphire paste shoe buckles made by London silversmith Matthew Boulton for Sag Harbor resident Henry Packard Dering, America's first customs officer. The circa 1830 dresser also holds a collection of antique autograph books and bound volumes that come from local collections or relate to the region.*

ABOVE: *In a corner of the bedroom is a group of three Dominy stands, 1810–30, known as "the sisters" because they are crafted with similar turnings, spider legs and swept corners typical of the late Federal/early Empire period.*

OPPOSITE: *The lavender guest room is decorated invitingly with a collection of old shells, some from the China sea, an early nineteenth-century portrait by Abraham Dominy Tuthill, and curiosity domes filled with bouquets made from tiny shells. A collection of etchings of local scenes sits atop a headboard fashioned from a Federal-style mantelpiece.*

ABOVE: *Graphic designer Eric Mueller created this compact arrangement of miniature artwork, objects, and memorabilia. Featuring locally collected folk art pieces, watercolor portraits of the Foster family, an Annie Cooper Boyd view of Sag Harbor, and memorabilia from visiting friends, the montage is a celebration of place and time.*

High Rise Antiques

The prospect of downsizing is daunting for avid collectors. When Stephanie and Bill Reeves swapped their Tudor-style home in Atlanta for a condominium half its size, they definitely felt the pinch. To add to the challenge, the condominium is in a 1960s building with floor-to-ceiling windows that lend it a distinctly modern air. But by the time the Reeveses had installed a well-curated selection of art, furniture, and decorative miscellany, the apartment bore a greater resemblance to a nineteenth-century London gentleman's flat or a Boston Brahmin's townhouse than to a contemporary high-rise condo.

"We couldn't keep everything," Stephanie admits, "so it came down to choosing what we loved most." And that, it turned out, was rather a lot, including the two sofas, three armchairs, seven tables of various sizes and styles, and twelve portraits that furnish the living room. With pieces from England, France, America, and China that range in period from the eighteenth to the twentieth century, the room's contents might easily have collided in a design disaster. Instead, they coexist peacefully in an elegant and even understated way. According to the Reeveses, the secret is that their former residence was decorated in a unified palette of taupe, gold, and brown. "All the furniture works together," Stephanie observes, "even though it didn't all come from the same room." The same can be said of the portraits, previously displayed in many rooms of a house and now hanging on a single wall. Despite variety in style, size, and framing, they work together in a cohesive composition of black, brown, ivory, and gilt.

"We displayed the portraits as if they were in a bigger room," Bill Reeves explains. "As a result, the space looks bigger." This is one of several strategies that make their favorite possessions fit gracefully in the new space. Another was not to shy away from using larger pieces. Among these were two sideboards, neither of which fit in the dining room. Stephanie put one in the living room where it creates a handsome focal point and brackets an American neo-classical sofa arranged at the far end of the space. The other

accents a library adjoining the room, with a seven-foot-tall Chinese screen as a divider.

"The most difficult thing about the move was deciding how many accessories to take," recalls Stephanie, who, with her husband, collects silver, English pottery, French porcelain, maps and prints, portrait miniatures, and silhouettes—among other things. A significant number found their way into the library, where built-in bookcases provide perfectly scaled compartments for displaying them in combination with antique books. Staffordshire poodles sit on one shelf, silhouetted against a row of green and gold bindings. In another compartment, an easel placed on top of a diminutive Empire chest of drawers supports a portrait miniature. Each shelf is full, but because everything is arranged with an eye for balance and color, there's no sense of clutter.

The same sleight of hand is at work in the bedroom, where twenty-two framed silhouettes hang on a small wall. Like the living room portraits, they vary in shape and size, but ultimately this became an advantage. "We massed them above the chest as if they were a single painting," says Bill. "The differences in their shapes and the finish of their frames made the composition interesting." This talent for creating dynamic wall compositions also finds expression in the kitchen, where brown-and-white transferware is mounted along with contemporary watercolors above an English tea table.

"Basically, we collect things that we love," Bill explains.

"They don't have to fall into certain categories. We just like things that are authentic and unique, that have character, or suggest a time or place. When these are the things you love, they will work any place."

OPPOSITE: *Old Paris porcelain pieces create an elegant pattern-on-pattern effect when arranged on an English Regency game table placed before a nineteenth-century Chinoiserie screen.*

The living room demonstrates the principle that putting several large pieces of furniture in a small room or decorating a wall with a tightly composed arrangement of similar objects creates the illusion of space. The glass wall enlarges the room visually, as well, and draws attention to the graceful lines of the American neoclassical sofa silhouetted against it. Although the furnishings encompass a wide range of styles, they work well together, thanks to a unifying palette of gold, beige, and brown.

LEFT AND ABOVE: *The library is small, but it has all the necessary ingredients—plenty of books, a comfortable sofa, a generously sized coffee table, and reading lamps, including an alabaster table lamp and a floor lamp adapted from an antique pole stand. The tight composition of French hand-colored engraved maps above the sofa makes a strong, but orderly, statement. A pillow made from a fragment of an eighteenth-century Aubusson carpet and a Turkish rug with burnished tones bring color into the overall neutral palette.*

ABOVE AND OPPOSITE: *A late-nineteenth-century English sideboard marks the entrance to the dining room. Delicate sconces hang above table lamps and a bull's-eye mirror surmounts a portrait in a dense but intriguing wall composition. Collections of small silver objects and antique miniature books rest on a sideboard dominated by a nineteenth-century gilded weathervane on a contemporary base.*

ABOVE: *A built-in bookcase designed with shelves of varying height to accommodate books of different dimensions provides display space for decorative objects, including Staffordshire poodles, English yellowware lion masks, and portrait miniatures.*

OPPOSITE: *From their large collection of English brown-and-white transfer ware, the Reeveses chose a selection of the hard-to-find William Penn Treaty series to display in their kitchen. These are artfully combined with contemporary watercolors by Atlanta artist Jeffrey Adler. The arrangement hangs above a mahogany tea table garnished with a lamp made from a tole samovar and flanked by Hepplewhite chairs.*

OPPOSITE: *The dining room is furnished with Anglo-Indian chairs purchased in Mumbai, a water-gilded Belgian chandelier, and an English mahogany secretary displaying a collection of silver hollowware. One wall is decorated with framed engravings of similar hollowware pieces from what the Reeveses describe as the nineteenth-century equivalent of a silversmith's catalog.*

ABOVE: *A Chinese export "lazy Susan" holds an American etched-glass eggnog bowl surrounded by cut-glass finger bowls and contemporary mercury-glass votives. Made from rosewood and ornamented with ivory pulls, the "lazy Susan" provides an arresting centerpiece marrying form, function, and beauty.*

Material History

Passionate collectors of houses and all that goes in them, Joy Lewis and her late husband, Robert Lewis, describe their approach to restoration as bonding down to the seventh layer.

"We bring together layers of locally relevant furniture, art, artifacts, and ephemera— all informed by research we've conducted in local historical societies."

To Joy and her husband, these relics are not only things to gaze at and touch, but also tangible reminders of the whaling and China trade booms that shaped the economy and cultural life of Long Island's North Fork. Many such objects fill the rooms of the couple's third and final Sag Harbor residence.

Composed of remnants of a small eighteenth-century farmhouse and a large Greek Revival addition built in the early nineteenth century for ship owner and financier Charles T. Dering, the house itself tells a tale, tracing the area's shifting economy from agriculture to whaling and international trade. While some owners of old houses would be satisfied with this degree of background information, for the Lewises, it was merely the beginning. "We researched everything we could about the house," says Joy, including the names and dates of its previous residents and logs and crew lists from Dering's ships.

This is just one of many particulars that weave webs of connections among objects in the collection. In the portrait of Samuel L'Hommedieu, another Sylvester descendant and Sag Harbor resident, the sitter's hand rests on what is thought to be an volume of *Fifteen Sermons by George Whitefield, A.B.*—a copy of which sits on the table beneath the painting. The Old Squire, as he was known, sits in a chair by East Hampton furniture maker Nathaniel Dominy, which bears a close resemblance to a pair of Dominy great chairs the Lewises acquired. Soon after they bought the house, the couple discovered that Dominy had also made the newel post for the stair banister.

In spite of the profusion of objects, the rooms are remarkably ordered and restrained. This is partially attributable to Robert Lewis, an interior designer who grew up among modernists (Eliel and Eero Saarinen were family friends) and later became fascinated with neoclassical styles. His room for the Kips Bay show house in 1986 was informed by Thomas Jefferson's taste and ideals. Several objects from the room found their way to this house, including casts of the Houdon busts Jefferson kept in his breakfast room. Neoclassical pieces in the Sag Harbor living room, including a New England Sheraton sofa, a New York silver tea service, c. 1800, and American klismos chairs, reflect the influence of ancient Greece on Jefferson's new democracy.

Together, the contents of the house provide a compelling portrait of a place and the nation to which it belongs, as well as of a specific era when sailors hunted whales and travelled to China, furniture makers mined classical forms, and explorers and artists catalogued their country's contents. A collection of ornithological prints by Alexander Wilson hanging in the upstairs hall illustrates that point. When Joy and Robert were reading a book about Jefferson, they discovered an excerpt of a letter from Jefferson to Louis and Clark commanding them to keep alive a magpie captured in Indian Territory, "so on your return, Wilson may paint it," he wrote. "We ran upstairs to see if we had the magpie, and there he was," Joy recalls. "That is what material culture is all about. It gives up the juice of history, so we can feel something and not just intellectualize it with words."

OPPOSITE: *A poignant mourning portrait attributed to Long Island painter Shepard Alonzo Mount memorializes a boy who was struck down by a passing wagon in 1837.*

OPPOSITE: *A handsome banister terminates with a newel post made by Nathaniel Dominy V of the prominent East Hampton furniture-making family. The entrance hall is filled with local artifacts including a lantern of free-blown, etched glass originally fueled by whale oil, leather fire buckets, and canes with sailor-carved handles.*

ABOVE: *A collection of prints depicting American birds is the work of Scottish ornithologist Alexander Wilson, a contemporary of John James Audubon.*

OPPOSITE: *A study in neoclassical order and elegance, the parlor is decorated with an early-nineteenth-century drum-top table, a Sheraton sofa, c. 1810–20, and a contemporaneous mahogany-veneer table with a hinged lid that opens to a leather writing surface. To avoid period-style stiffness, the Lewises added a coir rug, which, in Joy's words, "salts down" the formality of the room.*

ABOVE: *On the dining room mantel, a drapery pin shaped like a lotus blossom echoes the gilded carvings of the Empire mirror above and sits comfortably with ammonite shells. Antique glass Christmas ornaments fill the Old Paris pedestal basket.*

ABOVE: *A display of whaling paraphernalia including whale's tooth scrimshaw, pointed fids used for untying knots in rigging, and "whimsies" carved by sailors for children and lady friends are arranged on ocean-green baize.*

PRECEDING SPREAD: *The dining room's centerpiece is a classical mahogany table, c. 1820, surrounded by saber-leg klismos chairs. Four plaster busts, casts of Jean-Antoine Houdon's portraits of American statesmen, are installed at one end of the room along with a New Jersey neo-classical sideboard with hairy paw feet.*

OPPOSITE: *A New York Empire breakfront cabinet with a pullout butler's desk holds a collection of antique books, many of which came from local family libraries. One of the most fascinating is a 1767 Long Island journal that describes life during the whaling and China Trade era.*

ABOVE: *The master bedroom is home to a pair of portraits by Abraham Tuthill, a Long Island-born artist who studied under Benjamin West and earned the moniker "Portrait Painter in the Young Republic." The room also includes a rare Dominy toilet table and, on top of an American Empire chest of drawers, a ship model and an admiral's hat from the War of 1812.*

ABOVE: *A period model of the early nineteenth-century Sag Harbor whaleship Fanny was fashioned with whalebone trim and twisted silk sheets by a sailor.*

199

Time and Time Again

Three generations of antiques dealers—each with a different expertise—share quarters in a Connecticut house and barn built around 1780. The property came into the family in the 1970s when Gloria and Don Buckley, dealers in American Queen Anne and William and Mary furniture, acquired it, living in the handsome Federal house and used the adjoining ell and carriage shed as their shop. They filled their private rooms with same furniture they sold—banister-back chairs with curly crests, a William and Mary highboy with ball feet, and a maple slant-front desk with a thin red wash.

"I love American William and Mary furniture," says Gloria. "It has so much personality."

The Buckleys' granddaughter Chloë Rohn, now a dealer in primitive American antiques, remembers visiting the house as a child. While her parents Fritz and Dana Rohn traveled abroad, buying pieces for their own antiques business, Chloë and her sister often stayed with their grandmother, absorbing the deep sense of history conveyed by the house and its contents. Today Gloria Buckley lives in the ell and converted carriage shed, the Rohns are in the main house, and Chloë has a loft—in the literal meaning of the word—in the nearby barn.

As a result, the colonial American pieces have migrated to the ell and converted carriage shed and European antiques have gained a foothold in the main house. The living room is still painted the same moleskin brown Gloria chose, but the furnishings include an Italian *cassone* dating from the fifteenth or sixteenth century, an eighteenth-century Italian triptych of the Madonna and Child, and late-sixteenth-century Deftware on the mantel. The front hall illustrates a range of interests, juxtaposing an eighteenth-century Swedish chair and a 1675 English oak court cupboard displaying a Chinese carved wood goose, a Spanish colonial figure of Saint Michael, and a portion of the couple's extensive collection of shells.

Like her daughter and son-in-law, Buckley is not averse to collecting objects outside her primary focus. In her living room a seventeenth-century English chest displays with English hourglasses and a bronze sundial marked Londini 1693. Explaining her attraction to the antique timepieces, Gloria says, "I love the whole idea of time," echoing a sentiment shared by most passionate collectors. In the adjoining room, which serves both as Gloria's kitchen and the family's dining room, the mantel is inscribed: "Old wood to burn. Old wine to drink. Old books to read. Old friends to trust." Chloë, who as a child turned over the old hour glasses and watched the sand trickle through, recalls her grandmother drawing her attention to these words, suggestive of the importance of keeping the past alive. "Time moves slowly here," she observes.

"Not much has changed. My grandparents moved in, my parents moved in, and now I live here, but so much has stayed the same."

OPPOSITE: *A collection of antique hourglasses and a seventeenth-century book sit on top of a 1680 English chest that retains vestiges of original red paint. Needlepoint pieces hanging above the chest depict King Charles I and his wife, Henrietta Maria.*

OPPOSITE: *Built with a kitchen hearth in 1789, Buckley's living room still includes a fireplace with a crane for heavy pots and a baking oven. At her suggestion, the floor was painted to simulate the black-and-white marble floors of English country houses. Although the high-backed Queen Anne–style upholstered chairs are reproductions, the rest of the furnishings, including the painted-wood chairs and gate-leg table date primarily from the William and Mary period.*

ABOVE: *An early eighteenth-century portrait hangs above an American William and Mary slant-front desk covered with a thin wash of red paint, originally intended to brighten dimly lit colonial interiors.*

ABOVE: *An early eighteenth-century English portrait hangs above an American William and Mary chest of drawers. Displayed nearby, a satin vest of the same period brings history to life for its present-day owner.*

ABOVE RIGHT: *Eighteenth-century needlepoint slips, embellishments intended for decorative bed hangings, are mounted on indigo-dyed linen and arranged above the bedside table. The antique mohair dogs were a gift from Buckley's daughter.*

OPPOSITE: *A seventeenth-century crewelwork curtain from England, or possibly France, hangs at the head of Buckley's bed. Its rich blue is echoed by the bed cover and hangings, as well as the rug and upholstered stool. Colorful passementerie and the bed hangings' gold trim brighten the monochromatic scheme.*

RIGHT AND ABOVE: *Simple paneling in the Rohns' living room provides a quiet backdrop for European pieces including Delftware, an eighteenth-century Italian devotional triptych painted in the fifteenth-century manner, a copy of a Rubens painting and a primitive Italian table. Across the room, English and Italian busts garnish a fourteenth- or fifteenth-century Italian cassone with rare figural marquetry inherited by Fritz from his grandparents.*

PRECEDING SPREAD: *The large kitchen, dating from the late eighteenth century, now also serves as the family dining room. Eighteenth-century ladderback chairs surround a reproduction table illuminated by a chandelier made by a contemporary tinsmith. American pewter plates and English measures decorate the circa 1910 mantelpiece added after a kitchen fire.*

ABOVE AND OPPOSITE: *A late nineteenth-century Czech table with cabriole legs and an American spool-leg table of the same period furnish the kitchen in Chloe Rohn's barn dwelling. In the dining area, paintings by early-twentieth-century Connecticut artist Jessie Goodwin Preston surround an eighteenth-century oak Welsh dresser base and an American pine farmhouse table.*

Resources

ANTIQUES

Marvin Alexander Antique and Fine Reproduction Lighting
New York
marvinalexanderinc.com

Ann-Morris Antiques
New York
ann-morris.com

The Antiques Shop
Bridgehampton, New York
631.537.3838

Ardgowan Antiques
Inverkip, Scotland
ardgowanantiques.co.uk

Balzac Antiques
New Orleans
balzacantiques.com

Black Sheep Antiques
Harpersville, Alabama
blacksheepantiquesal.com

Bardith, Ltd.
New York
bardith.com

Ceylon et Cie
Dallas
ceylonetcie.com

East & Orient Company
Dallas
eastandorient.com

Elephant's Trunk Country Flea Market
New Milford, Connecticut
etflea.com

Kim Faison Antiques
Richmond, Virginia
kimfaisonantiques.com

W. Gardner Antiques
Houston, Texas
wgardnerltd.com

Interiors Market
Atlanta
Interiorsmarket.com

Jennings & Rohn Antiques
Woodbury, Connecticut, and Millerton, New York
jenningsandrohnantiques.com

Keil's Antiques
New Orleans
keilsantiques.com

Litchfield County Auctions
Litchfield, Connecticut
litchfieldcountyauctions.com

Moss Antiques
New Orleans
mossantiques.com

Mac Maison, Ltd.
New Orleans
macmaisonantiquesneworleans.com

Pittet Architecturals
Dallas
pittetarch.com

Fritz Porter
Charleston, South Carolina
fritzporter.com

John Rosselli Antiques
New York
johnrosselliantiques.com

Sage Street Antiques
Sag Harbor, New York
631.725.4036

Scott Antique Markets
Atlanta
scottantiquemarket.com

South Bay Auctions
East Moriches, New York
southbayauctions.com

Spencer Swaffer Antiques
Arundel, UK
spencerswaffer.com

The Stalls
Atlanta
thestalls.com

Brown & Co.
Dallas
brownandcoantiques.com

CK Swan
Highlands, North Carolina
ckswan.com

Uptowner Antiques
New Orleans
504.891.7700

Wallace Gallery
East Hampton, New York
631.329.4516

Yard Sale Antiques
East Hampton, New York
631.324.7048

ARCHITECTURAL SERVICES

Brad Kelly & Associates
BradKellyAssociates.com

Robertson Partners
robertsonpartners.net

Douglas C. Wright Architects
dcwarchitects.com

INTERIOR DESIGN

Florence de Dampierre
Florencededampierre.com

Susan Ferrier
McAlpine Booth & Ferrier Interiors
mcalpineboothferrier.com

Beverly Field
beverlyfieldinteriors@live.com

Mary McCollister Finch
Mary McCollister
& Company
marymcco@aol.com

Fawn Galli Interiors
fawngalli.com

Annie Kelly Art & Design
anniekelly.net

Mary Evelyn Interiors
maryevelyn.com

Nancy Price Interiors
nancypriceinteriors.com

LIGHTING
Circa Lighting
circalighting.com

**Edgar Reeves Lighting
and Antiques**
Atlanta
edgar-reeves.com

Yang's Double Happiness
Dallas
lampsdallas.com

FLORAL AND
EVENT DESIGN
Loot Vintage Rentals
Austin, Texas
lootvintagerentals.com

Rosehip Flora
Austin, Texas
rosehipflora.com

Jan Miller
Birmingham, Alabama
304.201.3116
janbmiller@gmail.com

Flower magazine
flowermag.com

TEXTILES AND
WALLPAPER
Brunschwig & Fils
brunschwig.com

Clarence House
clarencehouse.com

Colefax and Fowler
Colefax.com

Cowtan & Tout
Cowtan.com

The Fabric Studio
Litchfield, Connecticut
860.567.7736

Lisa Fine Textiles
lisafinetextiles.com

Fortuny
fortuny.com

Keivan Woven Arts
Atlanta
keivanwovenarts.com

Scalamandre
New York
scalamandre.com

CONTEMPORARY
FURNISHINGS
Ellouise Abbott
Dallas and Houston
ellouiseabbot.com

Walter Culp and Associates
Dallas and Houston
culpassociates.com

Scott + Cooner
Dallas and Austin
scottcooner.com

**David Sutherland
Showroom**
New York, Chicago, Houston,
Dallas, Los Angeles
Davidsutherlandshowroom.com

Acknowledgments

This book would not exist without the help and support of many people, including Gianfranco Monacelli and Elizabeth White of The Monacelli Press. Elizabeth's enthusiasm and guidance has been essential from the very beginning to the utter end. Thanks as well to Michael Vagnetti, production director at Monacelli, and designer Jena Sher, who have created such a beautiful volume.

Much gratitude is also offered to the featured homeowners who shared their houses and possessions with me. Thank you for teaching us how to live beautifully and creatively with heirlooms and antiques. Special thanks are due to those whose homes are not featured, but who allowed me to photograph aspects of their graceful way of living with antiques, including Rhoda Brimberry and Anna Crelia of Loot Vintage Rentals in Austin, Texas, Teri and Mose Bond, Madeline and Fred Knox, Nancy Price, Lisa Fine, Ashley Spotswood, and Margot Shaw, publisher of Flower magazine. And finally, a huge sigh of gratitude goes out to all my friends and family who helped me create a book during a most challenging year, including Elizabeth Shreve Ryan, Nancy Ryan, Frances Portis, Maggie Cook, Ricard and Mateu Bordas, Marty and Charles Cornwall, Norman and Joane Askins, and the rest. You know who you are and how much I love you.

I dedicate this book to Elizabeth Shreve Ryan, extraordinary mother and memory keeper.

Library of Congress Control Number
2015952730
ISBN 978-158093-439-8

Designed by Jena Sher

The Monacelli Press
236 West 27th Street
New York, New York 10001

Printed in Singapore